Berlitz®

Intermediate
French

Course Book

Berlitz Publishing

New York   Munich   Singapore

INTERMEDIATE FRENCH

Contacting the Editors
Every effort has been made to provide accurate information in this publication, but changes are inevitable. The publisher cannot be responsible for any resulting loss, inconvenience or injury. We would appreciate it if readers would call our attention to any errors or outdated information by contacting Berlitz Publishing, 193 Morris Avenue, Springfield, NJ 07081, USA.
Fax: 1-908-206-1103, email: comments@berlitzbooks.com

Printed in China, April 2008

Text: Rosi McNab
Editorial: Christine Frohly, Sheryl Olinsky Borg, Juergen Lorenz, Lorraine Sova, Dominique Wenzel, Piotr Brynczka, Diane Gigantino
Production: Steve Maher, Wee Design Group, Molly Pike Riccardi, Kent Wilkinson
Audio Producer: RPL, Paul Ruben Productions
Cover Design: Claudia Petrilli
Interior Design: Max Crandall
Illustrations: Max Crandall, Mona Daly, Elise Dodeles, Andy Levine, Chris Reed, Isabelle Verret, Guy Ruggiero
Maps: MAGELLAN Geographix, Parrot Graphics
Cover Photos: © MedioImages/photodisc/age fotostock; © rubberball/age fotostock; © Image Source Pink/Alamy; © 2007 Jupiterimages Corporation

Contents

Unit **1** is about everyday life. You will become familiar with the language you need to know in order to:

- talk about your home life
- say what you usually do during the weekend
- say what you have done, using the past tense

La vie quotidienne

Word Bank

le beurre	butter
les céréales f.pl.	breakfast cereal
la confiture	jam, jelly
le lait	milk
la margarine	margarine
le miel	honey
l'œuf m.	egg
le pain	bread
la tartine	slice of bread with butter or jam
la tasse	cup
le yaourt	yogurt
le week-end	weekend
jusqu'à	until
mais	but
normalement	usually
quelquefois	sometimes
toujours	always
vers	about (of time)
se réveiller	to wake up

réveiller	to wake someone else
se lever	to get up
lever	to lift/raise
se laver	to get washed
laver	to wash something/ someone else
s'habiller	to get dressed
habiller	to dress someone else
se raser	to shave (oneself)
raser	to shave someone else
*boire	to drink
faire la grasse matinée	to sleep in (lit: do a "fat" morning)
faire du jogging	to go jogging
prendre une douche	to take a shower
prendre un bain	to take a bath
prendre le petit déjeuner	to have breakfast
manger	to eat
rentrer	to go home
sécher	to dry

Que faites-vous le samedi matin?

What are you doing on Saturday morning?

RECORDING
1.

Listen to these people saying when they get up on a Saturday. Then match the number of the interview with the right clock. Remember, children in France usually go to school on Saturday morning so families often have to get up early, as usual.

RECORDING
2.

Listen to Lucien describing what he normally does on a Saturday. Number the pictures in the right order.

3.

Que fait Aurélie? *Listen and match the pictures with the phrases that describe what she is doing.*

a.

c.

b.

d.

e.

Elle prend une douche.

Elle prend son petit déjeuner.

Elle se lève.

Elle se réveille.

Elle se sèche les cheveux.

4.

Listen to Thomas describing what he usually does and what he sometimes does in the morning. Fill in the missing words.

a. _____ je me lève à sept heures, mais
_____ je me lève à six heures.

b. _____ je prends une douche, mais
_____ je fais du jogging.

c. _____ je ne prends pas de petit
déjeuner, mais _____ je mange une
tartine.

d. _____ je pars à huit heures, mais
_____ je pars à sept heures.

normalement   *usually*
quelquefois   *sometimes*

5. *What do these people eat for breakfast? Listen and put the right number beside each picture.*

a.   b.   c.

d.   e.

Je mange du/de la/des …	*I eat (some) …*
Je ne mange rien.	*I don't eat anything.*
Je bois du/de la …	*I drink (some) …*
Je ne bois rien.	*I don't drink anything.*
Je ne prends pas de petit déjeuner.	*I don't have breakfast.*

6. **A vous!** *How would you tell Sylvie what you do on Saturday morning? Complete these sentences about your usual routine.*

a. Normalement je me lève à _____.

b. Quelquefois je _____.

c. Normalement je prends/je ne prends pas de _____.

d. Quelquefois je prends/je ne prends pas de _____.

Pronunciation

RECORDING

Listen to Sylvie saying the parts of **s'appeler** *and* **se lever**. *Notice the different sound in the* **nous** *and* **vous** *forms of the verb. Repeat them after her, then practice repeating the question forms.*

Comment t'appelles-tu? *or* **Comment tu t'appelles?**

Comment vous appelez-vous? *or* **Comment vous vous appelez?**

A quelle heure te lèves-tu? *or* **A quelle heure tu te lèves?**

A quelle heure vous levez-vous? *or* **A quelle heure vous vous levez?**

Close-up

Reflexive verbs

You have already met one reflexive verb: **s'appeler**—*to be called (lit: to call oneself).*

The verb **lever** *means to lift, but* **se lever** *is to lift yourself, in other words, to get up.*

Laver *means to wash, but* **se laver** *means to wash yourself or get washed, and so on.*

s'appeler

je m'appelle	nous nous appelons
tu t'appelles	vous vous appelez
il s'appelle	ils s'appellent
elle s'appelle	elles s'appellent

se lever

je me lève	nous nous levons
tu te lèves	vous vous levez
il se lève	ils se lèvent
elle se lève	elles se lèvent

Note that **appeler** *doubles the* **l** *and* **lever** *takes a grave accent over the* **e** *in all except the* **nous** *and* **vous** *forms.*

The other reflexive verbs follow the regular **-er** *verb endings.*

Le week-end

The weekend

Word Bank

l'après-midi *m.*	afternoon	se faire bronzer	to sunbathe
le déjeuner	lunch	faire les courses	to do errands
le matin	morning	faire une balade en vélo	to go for a bike ride
le repas de midi	midday meal	faire un pique-nique	to go for a picnic
le soir	evening	faire de la planche (à voile)	to go windsurfing
à la campagne	in the country	faire une randonnée	to go for a hike/long walk
en été	in summer		
en hiver	in winter	faire du sport	to play sports
alors	then	jouer au football	to play soccer
ou	or	jouer au tennis	to play tennis
puis	then/next	rester	to stay
si	if/whether	se reposer	to rest

RECORDING

1. *Listen to these people talking about how they spend the weekend. Decide who is speaking and put the right number from the recording by each picture.*

infirmière
professeur
secrétaire
boulanger
vendeuse
homme d'affaires

Vous savez …
You know …

C'est le jour le plus important.
It's the most important day.

avant d'aller au collège
before going to school

What do these people do on Sunday? Listen and find out.

S'il fait beau …
If it's nice …

S'il ne fait pas beau …
If it's not nice …

What are you being invited to do? Put the right number beside the pictures.

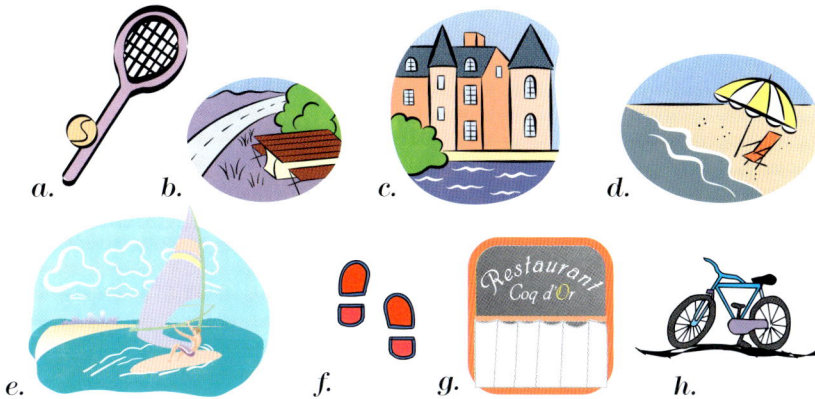

a.   b.   c.   d.

e.   f.   g.   h.

DidYouKnow?

The **pique-nique** is a part of French life. Many picnic areas can be found at the roadside and at regular distances along the highway. The ones on highways also have restrooms and are called **Aire**.

Voulez-vous vous joindre à nous?
Would you like to join us?

Quel beau temps!
What lovely weather!

Il y a juste le bon vent.
The wind is just right.

4. *Listen to these people saying what they would like to do. Write down the letter of the picture on the previous page that corresponds to the activity.*

a. Je voudrais aller au restaurant. J'ai faim.

b. Je voudrais faire de la planche.

c. Une randonnée, quelle bonne idée!

d. Je veux aller à la plage pour me faire bronzer un peu.

e. Qui veut jouer au tennis avec moi?

f. Je voudrais visiter le château.

J'ai faim.   *I'm hungry. (lit: I have hunger)*

5. **A vous!** *Now choose five activities and practice telling Sylvie that you would like to do them.*

Example: Je voudrais faire un pique-nique.

6. *Now it's your turn to invite a French friend. How would you suggest these activities? Practice saying your suggestion aloud!*

Example: Voulez-vous aller à la plage?

S'il fait beau on pourrait aller/jouer/faire …

S'il ne fait pas beau on pourrait rester/visiter …

*Did*You*Know*?

There are many beautiful **châteaux** *(castles) and stately homes to visit in France, and nearly every old town has at least one château. Many are well preserved, and some are still private homes. The* **Châteaux de la Loire** *(along the river Loire) are among some of the most famous.*

Pronunciation

Now practice saying these sentences, first as statements and then as questions. Listen carefully and try to imitate the rising intonation for questions and the falling intonation for statements.

Le matin on va en ville.   **Le matin on va en ville?**

L'après-midi on va à la plage.   **L'après-midi on va à la plage?**

Le soir on va au restaurant.   **Le soir on va au restaurant?**

Close-up

Rappel! **<u>On</u>** *with the* **il/elle** *form of the verb can be used in conversation to mean "one" or "we."*

Times of day

In French you do not need to use a word for "in" with times of day:

le matin	(in) the morning
Le matin on va en ville.	In the morning we go to town.
l'après-midi	(in) the afternoon
L'après-midi on va à la plage.	In the afternoon we go to the beach.
le soir	(in) the evening
Le soir on va au restaurant.	In the evening we go to the restaurant.

Qu'est-ce qu'on a fait hier?

What did we do yesterday?

Word Bank

l'anniversaire *m.*	*birthday*	pendant	*for, during*
le fast-food	*fast food restaurant*	faire les magasins	*to go shopping (lit: to "do" the shops)*
ensemble	*together*		
hier	*yesterday*	rencontrer	*to meet*

RECORDING 1.

Listen to these people describe what they did yesterday. Put the right numbers from the recording beside the pictures.

C'était mon anniversaire.   *It was my birthday.*

RECORDING 2.

Listen to Thierry describing what he did this morning. Fill in the clocks.

Qu'est-ce que Thierry a fait ce matin?

What did Thierry do this morning?

Listen to Sylvie talking about what she did yesterday morning, afternoon, and evening.

Put "A.M.," "P.M.," or "evening" by each picture.

4. **A vous!** *Now choose five sentences and complete them to say what you did yesterday morning.*

a. Je me suis réveillé(e) à _____.

b. Je me suis levé(e) à _____.

c. Je suis resté(e) au lit jusqu'à _____.

d. Pour le petit déjeuner j'ai mangé du/de la _____.

e. Pour le petit déjeuner je n'ai rien mangé mais j'ai bu _____.

f. J'ai quitté la maison à _____.

Pronunciation

Now let's practice saying what you have done using the perfect tense. Listen and repeat these phrases after Sylvie and think about what they mean.

je me suis réveillé(e)

je me suis levé(e)

je me suis lavé(e)

j'ai pris une douche

je me suis habillé(e)

je suis allé(e) en ville

j'ai mangé un croissant

j'ai bu un café

j'ai quitté la maison

Close-up

To say what you have done you use the perfect tense of the verb.

In most cases the perfect tense is formed by using the present tense of **avoir**, to have + the past participle (as in English):

J'<u>ai mangé</u> mon déjeuner.   I have eaten my lunch.

Some verbs form the present tense using **être**, to be + the past participle:

Je <u>suis allé(e)</u> en ville.   I have been to town. (lit: I am gone to town)

With verbs that take **être**, the past participle agrees with the subject. So, for the feminine you add **e** and for the plural you add **s**:

Mon père est allé en ville.	My father has gone to town.
Ma mère est all<u>ée</u> au bureau.	My mother has gone to the office.
Mes frères sont all<u>és</u> au match de foot.	My brothers have gone to the soccer game.
Mes sœurs sont all<u>ées</u> au cinéma.	My sisters have gone to the movies.

Close-up

Note that all the reflexive verbs take **être** and the past participle:

Je me suis levé(e).	*I got up.*	Elle s'est habillée.	*She got dressed.*
Il s'est rasé.	*He shaved.*	Vous vous êtes réveillés.	*You woke up.*

Forming the past participle:

a. **-er** *verbs—always take off the final* **er** *and add* **é**:

manger ⟶ mangé

b. **-re** *verbs—usually take off the final* **re** *and add* **u**:

répondre ⟶ répondu

c. **-ir** *verbs—usually take off the final* **r**:

finir ⟶ fini

Just as in English there are many irregular past participles and these do need to be learned.

The most common ones are:

avoir—*to have* — eu
J'ai <u>eu</u> la visite de ... — *I (have) had a visit from ...*

être—*to be* — été
J'ai <u>été</u> à Marseille. — *I have been to Marseilles.*

boire—*to drink* — bu
J'ai <u>bu</u> du vin rouge. — *I have drunk/I drank some red wine.*

faire—*to do* — fait
J'ai <u>fait</u> la vaisselle. — *I have done/I did the dishes.*

lire—*to read* — lu
J'ai <u>lu</u> le journal. — *I (have) read the newspaper.*

mettre—*to put* — mis
J'ai <u>mis</u> le bol sur la table. — *I (have) put the bowl on the table.*

ouvrir—*to open* — ouvert
J'ai <u>ouvert</u> le paquet. — *I (have) opened the packet.*

prendre—*to take* — pris
J'ai <u>pris</u> un bain. — *I have taken/I took a bath.*

recevoir—*to receive* — reçu
J'ai <u>reçu</u> une lettre. — *I (have) received a letter.*

Some **-ir** verbs take **u** in the past participle:

venir—*to come* — venu
Il est <u>venu</u> en retard. — *He has come/He came late.*

voir—*to see* — vu
Il a déjà <u>vu</u> le film. — *He's already seen the movie.*

vouloir—*to want* — voulu
J'ai <u>voulu</u> ... — *I wanted ...*

If this all seems very complicated, don't worry. The parts you need most will all be explained again each time you need to use the perfect tense.

Checkpoints

Use the check list to test what you've learned in this unit and review anything you're not sure of.

Can you ... ?

	Yes	No
● *say what time you normally wake up* .... Normalement je me réveille à ... heures.	❏	❏
● *say what you eat for breakfast* .... Je mange du/de la/des ...	❏	❏
● *say you don't eat anything* .... Je ne mange rien.	❏	❏
● *say what you drink* .... Je bois du/de la ...	❏	❏
● *say you don't eat breakfast* .... Je ne prends pas de petit déjeuner.	❏	❏
● *say in the morning* .... le matin	❏	❏
● *say in the afternoon* .... l'après-midi	❏	❏
● *say in the evening* .... le soir	❏	❏
● *say you would like to play tennis* .... Je voudrais jouer au tennis.	❏	❏
● *say you would like to go to the beach* .... Je voudrais aller à la plage.	❏	❏
● *suggest what you could do if it is nice* .... S'il fait beau on pourrait ...	❏	❏
● *suggest what you could do if it isn't nice* .... S'il ne fait pas beau on pourrait ...	❏	❏
● *say you could go to the movies* .... On pourrait aller au cinéma.	❏	❏
● *say you could go to a restaurant* .... On pourrait aller au restaurant.	❏	❏
● *use the perfect tense to say when you woke up* .... Je me suis réveillé(e) à ... heures.	❏	❏
● *use the perfect tense to say when you got up* .... Je me suis levé(e) à ... heures.	❏	❏

Can you ... ?	Yes	No
• say what you ate for breakfast	☐	☐
Pour le petit déjeuner j'ai mangé du/de la/des ...		
• say what you drank	☐	☐
J'ai bu ...		
• say when you left home	☐	☐
J'ai quitté la maison à ... heures.		

Learning tips

Where you see an accent circonflexe try adding an "s" after the vowel to see if it will help you to find related words in English:

château	*castle*
pâté	*paste*
arrêt	*arrest (stop)*

Do you want to learn more?

Look through the sports section of a French-language newspaper. See how many of the sports have similar names in English and in French.

For more practice, see Extra! on page A1.

U nit 2 is about food and meals and also about not feeling well. After completing this unit you will be able to:

- talk about food and meals at home
- say what you like and dislike
- order meals in a restaurant
- say how something is made
- tell someone that you don't feel well

Boire et manger

2

les légumes *m.*	vegetables	les œufs *m.*	eggs
l'ail *m.*	garlic	le yaourt	yogurt
les carottes *f.pl.*	carrots	la viande	meat
le céleri	celery	l'agneau *m.*	lamb
les champignons *m.*	mushrooms	le bœuf	beef
le chou	cabbage	la dinde	turkey
le chou-fleur	cauliflower	le gibier	game meat
les haricots *m.*	beans	le jambon	ham
les oignons *m.*	onions	le porc	pork
les petits pois *m.*	peas	le poulet	chicken
les pommes de terre *f.*	potatoes	le ragoût	stew/casserole
les radis *m.*	radishes	le veau	veal
la salade	lettuce	la volaille	poultry
les tomates *f.*	tomatoes	les cuisses de grenouille *f.*	frogs' legs
les produits laitiers *m.*	dairy products		
la crème fraîche	cream	le dessert	dessert
le beurre	butter	les escargots *m.*	snails
le fromage	cheese	les noix *f.*	nuts
le lait	milk	le poisson	fish

Qu'est-ce que vous aimez manger?

What do you like to eat?

RECORDING 1.

Listen to these customers at a market stall. Which vegetables are they buying and in what quantities? What do you think they are going to make?

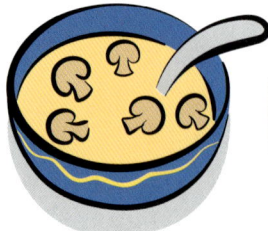

choucroute

soupe aux champignons

salade mixte

Now you choose some vegetables and practice asking for them in various quantities.

un kilo	1kg
un demi-kilo, une livre	½kg
deux cents grammes	200g
deux cent cinquante grammes	250g
cinq cents grammes	500g

RECORDING 2.

Listen and write down what meat each person likes to eat. Choose a suitable dish for each!

steak frites

blanquette de veau

salade niçoise

poulet rôti frites

Et vous, qu'est-ce que vous aimez comme viande?

Qu'est-ce que vous aimez comme viande?	*What sort of meat do you like?*
Je n'aime pas tellement …	*I don't really like …*
Je suis végétarien(ne).	*I'm a vegetarian.*
Ça manque de goût.	*It lacks taste/flavor.*
Je suis très steak frites.	*I am a great "steak and fries" person.*
le poulet rôti	*roast chicken*

RECORDING 3.

Listen and find out which speaker chooses which dessert.

tarte au citron
crème brûlée
gâteau au chocolat
glace aux fraises

Je suis allergique aux cacahuètes.
I am allergic to peanuts.

Je fais un régime.
I'm on a diet.

Ça me donne mal au cœur.
That gives me indigestion/That makes me sick to my stomach.

Je ne mange pas de choses sucrées.
I don't eat anything sweet.

Ça me fait grossir.
It makes me fat.

Je ne peux jamais résister à …
I can never resist …

A vous! *You have been invited to dinner and your hosts want to know what you like and don't like to eat. Tell them.*

J'aime …

Je n'aime pas tellement …

Je ne mange pas de …

Je suis très …

Je suis allergique à la/à l'/au/aux …

Sylvie is asking some people what they think of snails. Listen and check what they say.

Comment trouvez-vous les escargots?
What do you think of snails?

délicieux
delicious

curieux
strange

un goût particulier
a special taste

insipide
tasteless

bof!
not a lot (usually accompanied by a shrug of the shoulders)

beurk!
yuk!

dégoûtant!
disgusting!

A vous! *Practice asking a visitor what he or she likes.*

Aimez-vous … ?

Mangez-vous … ?

Préférez-vous … ?

Comment trouvez-vous … ?

Voulez-vous du/de la/des … ?

Did You Know?

If you are invited to a formal meal in a French restaurant or home you will probably be offered an apéritif first to prepare the palate, e.g., a Pernod or other aniseed-based drink or even a glass of champagne. The meal then traditionally consists of five courses:

Hors-d'œuvre: *a small starter of perhaps salad, paté, snails, or soup.*

Entrée: *usually a fish, cheese or egg dish.*

Le plat principal: *meat and vegetables.*

Le fromage: *cheese and bread.*

Le dessert *or* **un fruit**.

Note that the dessert is served after the cheese, with usually a strong black coffee to finish it off. Do you know how to ask for a decaffeinated coffee?
Un déca, s'il vous plaît.

Pronunciation

Practice saying these phrases after Sylvie and Jacques, paying particular attention to the pronunciation.

Le bœuf est délicieux.

Les escargots sont délicieux.

Le goût est curieux.

Les fromages sont curieux.

La tarte est délicieuse.

Les fraises sont délicieuses.

La glace est curieuse.

Les cuisses de grenouille sont curieuses.

Close-up

Toujours la politesse! (Being polite at the table.)

Rappel! *If you are offered something and want it, say* **"Oui"** *or* **"S'il vous plaît."** **"Merci"** *on its own means "No thank you."*

If you are full and don't want any more, you can say **"J'ai assez mangé,"** *I have eaten enough, or even* **"J'ai déjà trop mangé,"** *I have already eaten too much.* **"Je suis plein(e),"** *I am "full" is a slang way of saying you have had too much to drink (lit: I am tanked up) and should be avoided.*

Adjective agreement

	m.	f.
sing.	Le bœuf est bon.	La tarte est bonne.
pl.	Les escargots sont bons.	Les fraises sont bonnes.

Adjectives ending in **x** *don't change for the masculine plural:*

	m.	f.
sing.	Le bœuf est délicieux.	La tarte est délicieuse.
pl.	Les escargots sont délicieux.	Les fraises sont délicieuses.

Au restaurant

At the restaurant

Word Bank

les asperges *f.*	*asparagus*	la galette	*savory pancake*
l'assiette *f.*	*plate*	le pain	*bread*
la demi-bouteille	*half-bottle*	le poivre	*pepper*
le cendrier	*ashtray*	le repas	*meal*
le couteau	*knife*	le sel	*salt*
la crêpe	*pancake*	le sucre	*sugar*
la cuillère	*spoon*	là	*there*
la farine	*flour*	formidable	*super/fantastic*
de blé noir	*buckwheat*	rempli(e)	*filled*
complète	*whole wheat*	salé(e)	*salty/savory*
la fourchette	*fork*		

~ Le Bistro de la Gare ~

Menu à 12 euros

ENTRÉES
AU CHOIX:
La Bouillabaisse froide en gelée
La Salade veriée aux pignons de pin
Soupe du jour

VIANDES ET POISSONS
AU CHOIX:
La Suggestion du jour (avec supplément):
Suprême de volaille
Filet de poisson frais du Bistro
Le Coeur d'aloyau "sauce beouf"
Le steak au poivre

ACCOMPAGNEMENT DE LÉGUMES
AU CHOIX:
Les Pommes allumettes fraîches
Le Chou-fleur au gratin

FROMAGE OU DESSERT

Listen to the clerk at your hotel advising these tourists where to eat. Check the places she recommends.

J'ai faim.	I'm hungry.
Vous êtes pressés.	You are in a hurry.
à toute heure	all the time
pas grand-chose	nothing much
en quittant	leaving
un petit quelque chose	a little something
pas loin du tout	not far at all
à cette heure-ci	at this time (lit: at this hour here)

Listen to find out what these people order. Put the speaker's number beside the appropriate dish on the menu opposite.

3.

A vous! *Choose a meal for yourself and a friend and practice saying your order aloud.*

Je voudrais …	I would like …
pour moi	for me
pour lui/elle	for him/her

RECORDING 4.

Listen to find out what each customer is asking for or complaining about.

Je n'ai pas de …	I don't have a …
Avez-vous … ?	Do you have … ?
encore	more
Il n'y a pas de …	There isn't a …

RECORDING 5.

More practice in understanding spoken prices! Listen to find out what each check comes to, then put the number of the speaker by the appropriate total. Practice saying the numbers aloud.

€37,80   €35   €48,60   €59,20   €31,45

Pronunciation

RECORDING

More practice with numbers. Repeat these numbers after Sylvie:

9 18 27 36 45 54 63 72 81 90 99

Now repeat these numbers after Jacques:

5 10 15 20 25 30 35 40 45 50
55 60 65 70 75 80 85 90 95 100

Close-up

In French the verb **avoir**, to have, is used in certain expressions where in English the verb to be is used:

J'<u>ai</u> faim.
I am hungry.

<u>Avez</u>-vous faim?
Are you hungry?

J'<u>ai</u> soif.
I am thirsty.

<u>Avez</u>-vous soif?
Are you thirsty?

J'<u>ai</u> chaud.
I am hot.

<u>Avez</u>-vous chaud?
Are you hot?

J'<u>ai</u> froid.
I am cold.

<u>Avez</u>-vous froid?
Are you cold?

The **ne** is often omitted in spoken French:

J'ai pas de …	*I don't have a …* (je n'ai pas de)
J'sais pas.	*I don't know.* (je ne sais pas)
J'ai rien vu.	*I haven't seen anything.* (je n'ai rien vu)
C'est pas grave.	*It doesn't matter.*
	(ce n'est pas grave; *lit: it isn't serious*)

J'ai mal au cœur

I feel sick

Word Bank

le bras	*arm*		le dentiste	*dentist*
le cœur	*heart*		le médecin	*doctor*
le corps	*body*		le service des urgences	*emergency service*
les dents *f.*	*teeth*		les médicaments	*medicine*
le dos	*back*		l'ampoule *f.*	*blister*
le genou	*knee*		les analgésiques	*painkillers*
la gorge	*throat*		la crème antiseptique	*antiseptic cream*
la jambe	*leg*		la cuillère à soupe	*tablespoon*
la main	*hand*		la cuillerée à soupe	*a spoonful*
l'oreille *f.*	*ear*		le sirop	*syrup*
l'œil *m.* (les yeux *pl.*)	*eye*		le pansement	*bandage*
le pied	*foot*		les suppositoires *m.*	*suppositories*
le talon	*heel*		emmener	*to take (someone)*
la tête	*head*		prendre un rendez-vous	*to make an appointment*
le ventre	*stomach*		tousser	*to cough*

*Listen to these people and write down what is wrong
with them.*

Qu'est-ce qui vous arrive?	*What's wrong with you?*
J'ai mal à la/à l'/au/aux …	*My … hurt(s).*
J'ai mal aux dents.	*I have a toothache.*
J'ai de la fièvre.	*I have a temperature. (lit: fever)*
J'ai trop mangé.	*I've eaten too much.*
Je me suis fait mal à la/à l'/au/aux …	*I've hurt my …*

A vous! *Listen and practice saying what's wrong with you!*

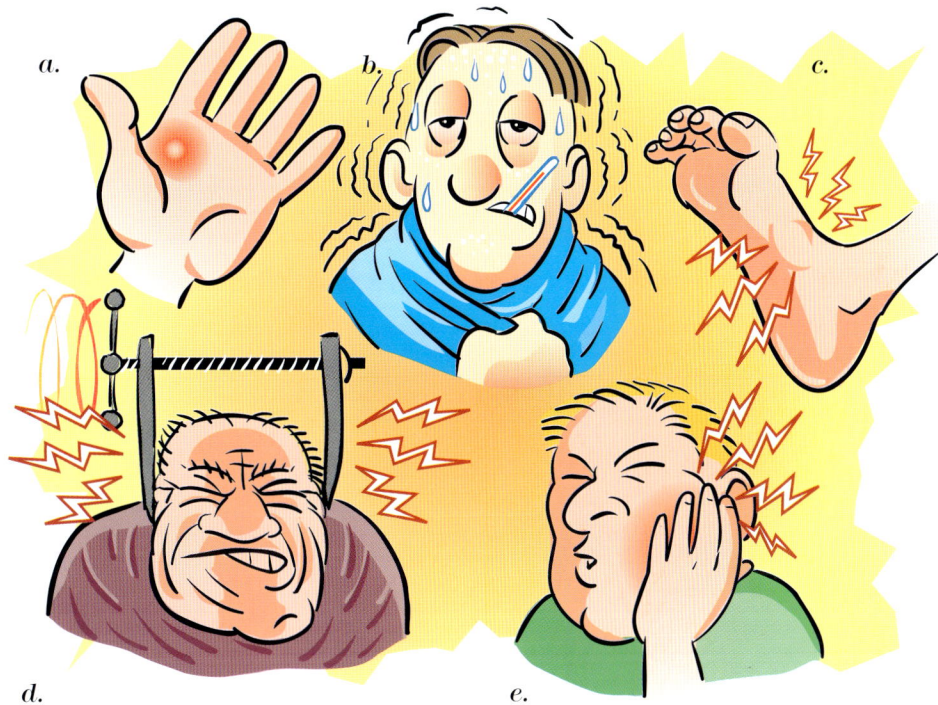

a.

b.

c.

d.

e.

*Listen and write down when these people have an
appointment. Listen again to check your answers.*

a.

b.

c.

d.

e.

Faites le numéro 15.	*Dial 15.*

Listen to this conversation in the doctor's waiting room. Write down what is wrong with each patient.

chez le médecin	*at the doctor's*
J'ai une grippe.	*I have the flu.*
J'ai de la toux/Je tousse.	*I have a cough.*
Je suis enrhumé(e).	*I have a cold.*
J'ai pris un coup de soleil.	*I have a sunburn.*
Je me suis coupé le doigt.	*I cut my finger.*
à cause du temps	*because of the weather*

A vous! *Now you ask for an appointment and say what is wrong with you.*

Je veux un rendez-vous avec le médecin/le dentiste.
I want an appointment with the doctor/dentist.

Je me suis cassé une dent.
I have broken a tooth.

J'ai perdu un plombage.
I have lost a filling.

Listen to the pharmacist at the drugstore. What remedy is she giving her customers and what instructions does she give? What do you think might be wrong with them?

Je vais vous donner des comprimés.
I'll give you some tablets.

Je vous propose …
I suggest (to you) …

Avez-vous quelque chose pour une grippe/un mal de gorge/un mal de tête?
Do you have something for the flu/a sore throat/a headache?

DidYouKnow?

To buy any medicines in France you have to go to a **pharmacie**. Medicines are not allowed to be sold elsewhere. The pharmacist is also fully qualified to prescribe medicines for most straightforward ailments, and will tell you if he or she thinks you need to see a doctor.

Pronunciation

Listen and repeat these phrases after Sylvie and Jacques.

J'ai mal au cœur.

Tu as mal au dos.

Il a mal à la tête.

Elle a mal aux oreilles.

Nous avons mal à la gorge.

Vous avez mal aux dents.

Ils ont mal aux pieds.

Elles ont mal aux yeux.

Et vous, qu'est-ce que vous avez?

Moi? Je n'ai rien, moi!

Close-up

Rappel!

à + le/la/les

m.	*f.*	*pl.*
à + le = <u>au</u>	<u>à la</u>	à + les = <u>aux</u>
J'ai mal <u>au</u> cœur.	J'ai mal <u>à la</u> gorge.	J'ai mal <u>aux</u> dents.

Perfect tense

*Most verbs take **avoir** in the perfect tense:*

J'ai perdu un plombage.   *I have lost a filling.*

*These verbs take **être**:*

aller—*to go*	venir—*to come*
arriver—*to arrive*	partir—*to leave*
entrer—*to enter*	sortir—*to go out*
monter—*to go up*	descendre—*to come down*
rester—*to stay*	tomber—*to fall down*

*All reflexive verbs take **être**:*

Je me suis levé(e).	*I got up.*
Il s'est coupé le doigt.	*He cut his finger.*
Nous nous sommes habillés.	*We got dressed.*
Ils se sont couchés.	*They went to bed.*

<u>en</u>—*of it/of them*

Vous <u>en</u> prenez deux.   *You take two (of them).*

Checkpoints

Use the check list to test what you've learned in this unit and review anything you're not sure of.

Can you ... ?

                                                                          Yes   No

- *ask for 1kg of potatoes* .... ❑ ...... ❑
  un kilo de pommes de terre

- *ask for 500g of cheese* .... ❑ ...... ❑
  cinq cents grammes de fromage

- *say what sort of meat you like* .... ❑ ...... ❑
  J'aime le porc/le bœuf/le poulet.

- *say you are vegetarian* .... ❑ ...... ❑
  Je suis végétarien(ne).

- *say you don't like something very much* .... ❑ ...... ❑
  Je n'aime pas tellement ...

- *say you are full* .... ❑ ...... ❑
  J'ai assez mangé.

- *say if you are on a diet* .... ❑ ...... ❑
  Je fais un régime.

- *say you are allergic to peanuts.* .... ❑ ...... ❑
  Je suis allergique aux cacahuètes.

- *say it's delicious* .... ❑ ...... ❑
  C'est délicieux!

- *ask if someone prefers chicken* .... ❑ ...... ❑
  Préférez-vous le poulet?

- *say you are hungry and thirsty* .... ❑ ...... ❑
  J'ai faim. J'ai soif.

- *order steak and fries* .... ❑ ...... ❑
  Un steak frites.

- *ask for some more bread* .... ❑ ...... ❑
  encore du pain

- *say you don't have a knife* .... ❑ ...... ❑
  Je n'ai pas de couteau.

- *say you don't want a dessert* .... ❑ ...... ❑
  pas de dessert

- *say you feel sick* .... ❑ ...... ❑
  J'ai mal au cœur.
  Je suis enrhumé(e).
  J'ai de la fièvre.

- *say you would like to make an appointment* . . . . ☐ . . . . . . ☐
  Je voudrais prendre un rendez-vous.

Learning tips

Listen to a family soap opera on television and notice how many "filler noises" are added. Listen again to the dialogs, or to a French film, and build up a list of useful "noises" to fill any gaps in a conversation or to give you time to think of what to say next. Here are a few to remember:

euh	*er*
hum	*um*
et alors	*and then/but*
mais voilà/et voilà	*(but/and) there you are*
et puis	*and then*
vous savez	*you know*
dis donc!	*well I never! (to express surprise)*
peut-être	*perhaps*
normalement/d'habitude	*usually*
ben	*well, er*
ouais	*yeah*
tiens!	*well!*

Do you want to learn more?

Many French-language housekeeping magazines have cooking recipes. If you can get hold of one, see how many of the ingredients you can identify. Also, some products you buy may have instructions or contents listed in French as well as in English on the packaging. The next time you're buying wine, keep a look out for French wines and study the labels to see how much information you can understand.

For more practice, see Extra! on page A2.

U nit 3 is about going on vacation. You will become familiar with the language you need to know in order to:

- say where you like to go on vacation
- and where you have been (using the past tense)
- say what you like to do
- and what you have done on your last vacation (using the past tense)
- find a place to stay and make a reservation

En vacances 3

Word Bank

le bord de la mer	*seaside*	le soleil	*the sun*
la campagne	*the country*	l'est	*east*
le camping	*camping/campsite*	le nord	*north*
les grandes vacances	*the summer vacation*	l'ouest	*west*
le groupe touristique	*tour group*	le sud	*south*
les lieux historiques	*historic sites*	les Antilles	*the Caribbean islands*
la mer	*the sea*	l'Orient	*the East*
la montagne	*the mountain(s)*	faire du tourisme	*to go sightseeing*
la plage	*the beach*		

Où allez-vous en vacances?

Where do you go on vacation?

1.

Where do these people like to spend their vacation? Write down the letter of the place each speaker prefers and say where you like to go.

a.

b.

c.

d.

J'aime aller …
I like to go …

DidYouKnow?

Les grandes vacances.
The summer vacation is also referred to as **la grande évasion**—*the great escape. In August in France almost everyone goes on vacation and Paris virtually closes down, except for foreign tourists. The majority of French people spend their holidays in France as the country has something to offer everyone and the weather can usually be relied on in summer to be hot and sunny. The vast majority still go to the seaside, where they stay on well-equipped campsites or in apartments or hotels. The next most popular vacation is* **le tourisme vert**—*holidays in the country.*

Listen to these people saying where they are going to go this year. Write down the letter of the region they are going to.

cette année   *this year*

These people are going further afield. This exercise is to help you become familiar with words that you would recognize if they were written down, but which are not always as easy to understand when spoken by a French person. Listen for these words and check them when you hear them.

les Antilles	Australie	la Martinique	New York
Londres	Los Angeles	Stratford	Sydney
l'Outback	Oxford	Washington	Japon
Las Vegas	walkabout	l'Orient	Tahiti
les Etats-Unis	le Grand Canyon		

Who are these people going with? Listen to find out.

ma famille

mes copains

mon petit ami/
mon copain

ma petite amie/
ma copine

mes enfants

Nous sommes quatre.	*There are four of us.*
mes copains	*my buddies*
mon copain/ma copine	*my boyfriend/my girlfriend*
tout(e) seul(e)	*alone*

Listen to Sylvie asking where these people went last year.

Où êtes-vous allé(e) l'année dernière?	*Where did you go last year?*
Je suis resté(e) à la maison.	*I stayed at home.*
comme toujours	*as usual*
On y va chaque année.	*We go there every year.*
vous savez …	*you know …*
les flirts	*flirts*
le fric	*dough/cash (slang word for money)*
le surf des neiges	*snowboarding*

6. **A vous!** *Answer the following questions.*

Où allez-vous cette année et avec qui?

Cette année je vais _____ avec _____.

Où êtes-vous allé(e) l'année dernière et avec qui?

L'année dernière je suis allé(e) _____ avec _____.

Pronunciation

RECORDING

The past participles usually sound the same in the masculine, feminine, singular, and plural. Listen to Sylvie and Jacques and repeat each phrase after them.

m.	f.
Je suis allé aux Etats-Unis.	Je suis allée à Miami.
Je suis resté en France.	Je suis restée à Paris.
Nous sommes allés en Angleterre.	Nous sommes allées à Londres.
Ils sont restés à la maison.	Elles sont restées en ville.

And now practice the letter "l" by repeating these phrases:

J'aime visiter les lieux historiques.

J'adore le soleil.

Je voudrais aller aux Antilles.

Je suis allé(e) en ville.

Il est tout seul.

Elle est toute seule.

Close-up

Rappel!

The word for "in"

a. *With feminine countries use* **en**: **en France**, **en Amérique**

b. *With the names of towns and cities use* **à**: **à Washington**, **à Tokyo**

c. *With masculine and plural countries use* **au**/**aux**:

à + le = au   J'habite au Canada.

à + les = aux   J'habite aux Etats-Unis.

The word for "my" also changes to agree with the word it precedes.

m.	f.	pl.
mon mari	ma femme	mes enfants
my husband	*my wife*	*my children*

Before feminine nouns that begin with a vowel, you use **mon**:

mon ami—*my (male) friend*   mon amie—*my (female) friend*

BUT

mon petit ami—*my boyfriend*   ma petite amie—*my girlfriend*

In conversation **on** *(one/we) is often used instead of* **nous** *(we). It is followed by the third person singular (***il/elle*** form) of the verb:*

on va/nous allons   *we are going*

on est allé/nous sommes allé(e)s   *we went*

on fait du camping/nous faisons du camping   *we go camping*

on a fait du camping/   *we went/have been camping*
nous avons fait du camping

Être + past participle agreement

With verbs that take **être** *in the perfect tense, the past participle agrees with the subject. So, for the feminine you add* **e** *and for the plural you add* **s**:

m.	f.
Je suis allé en France.	Je suis allée en France.
Nous sommes allés en France.	Nous sommes allées en France.

BUT

On est allé en France.   On est allé en France.

Qu'est-ce que vous aimez faire?

What do you like doing?

Word Bank

le canoë-kayak	*canoeing*	la tranquillité	*peace and quiet*
le chalet	*chalet*	les vacances de neige	*winter vacation*
le cheval	*horse*	la voile	*sailing*
le cyclisme	*cycling*	le volley	*volleyball*
l'équitation *f.*	*horse-back riding*	le VTT (vélo tout terrain)	*mountain biking*
l'escalade *f.*	*rock climbing*	adorer	*to love*
le foot	*soccer*	aimer	*to like*
le golf	*golf*	détester	*to hate*
le hockey sur glace	*ice hockey*	s'imaginer (galoper)	*to imagine oneself (galloping)*
le jogging	*jogging*		
la luge	*sledding*	préférer	*to prefer*
la natation	*swimming*	répondre (aux questions)	*to answer (questions)*
la neige	*snow*		
le parapente	*paragliding*	alors	*well/then*
le patin à glace	*ice skating*	même	*even*
la pêche (au brochet)	*(pike) fishing*	pendant	*during*
la planche à voile	*windsurfing*	quand	*when*
la plongée	*diving*	vraiment	*really*
le rafting	*rafting*	actif/active	*active*
la randonnée	*hiking*	affreux/affreuse	*awful*
le repos	*rest*	fantastique	*fantastic*
le ski	*skiing*	génial(e)	*great*
le ski nautique	*waterskiing*	reposant	*relaxing*
le ski alpin	*downhill skiing*	stupide	*stupid*
le ski de fond	*cross-country skiing*	superbe	*superb*

What do these people like doing? Listen and write down the activities they enjoy.

pendant les vacances	*during the vacation*
fana de (sport)	*(sport) fanatic/fan*
un peu	*a bit*
Vous le connaissez?	*Do you know it/him?*

And what do they dislike? Listen and find out.

Je suis paresseux/paresseuse.
I am lazy.

et tout ça
and all that

allongé(e) sur la plage
stretched out on the beach

C'est dangereux.
It's dangerous.

On risque de mourir d'un cancer.
You risk dying of cancer.

DidYouKnow?

More and more people are choosing to combine sport and relaxation by going on activity vacations. The most popular sports in France are **la pêche** and **le cyclisme**. The famous "Tour de France" is a 4,000 km cycle race which lasts three weeks and includes very difficult mountain sections in the Alps or Pyrenees. Other sports that are fast gaining popularity are **la planche à voile**, **la plongée**, **l'escalade**, **le VTT**, and **le ski**. A more sedate but by no means less popular sport is **la pétanque**, a form of bowling played outside, often in the town square.

Listen to Sylvie asking these people if they have ever tried paragliding. What do they think of it? Write down what they say.

Avez-vous jamais essayé de faire du parapente?	*Have you ever tried paragliding?*
une fois	*once*
deux fois	*twice*
plusieurs fois	*several times*
jamais	*never*
C'était …	*It was …*
quelque chose d'extra	*something great*

Now listen to find out what they would like to do.

Qu'est-ce que vous aimeriez faire?
What would you like to do?

J'aimerais (essayer)
I would like (to try)

Je voudrais bien (apprendre)
I would really like (to learn)

J'ai peur.
I'm afraid. (lit: I have fear)

Listen to find out what these people do on their winter vacation. Match the speaker with the appropriate picture.

A vous! *Prepare your own answers to the same questions.*

Qu'est-ce que vous aimez faire?

J'aime _____.

Et qu'est-ce que vous n'aimez pas faire?

Je n'aime pas _____.

Avez-vous jamais essayé de faire du parapente?

J'ai essayé _____ fois.

Avez-vous jamais fait du rafting?

Jamais.

Pronunciation

Practice asking the questions after Sylvie:

Qu'est-ce que vous aimez faire?

Et qu'est-ce que vous n'aimez pas faire?

Avez-vous jamais essayé de faire du parapente?

Now practice saying the parts of the verb **aimer,** *first in the affirmative, then in the negative. Notice how most parts of the verb just sound like the letter "M"!*

j'aime	**nous aimons**
tu aimes	**vous aimez**
il aime	**ils aiment**
elle aime	**elles aiment**

je n'aime pas	nous n'aimons pas
tu n'aimes pas	vous n'aimez pas
il n'aime pas	ils n'aiment pas
elle n'aime pas	elles n'aiment pas

And finally, practice saying:

j'aimerais	Aimeriez-vous?

Close-up

Say what you like and don't like and ask someone what he/she likes to do:

J'aime	I like
J'adore	I love
Je préfère	I prefer
Je n'aime pas	I don't like
Je déteste	I hate
Aimez-vous ... ?	Do you like ... ?
Préférez-vous ... ?	Do you prefer ... ?

Say what you would like to try and ask what someone would like to try:

J'aimerais essayer (de faire du parapente).

I'd like to try (paragliding).

Aimeriez-vous essayer (la luge)?

Would you like to try (sledding)?

Quel hôtel?

Which hotel?

Word Bank

l'auberge *f.*	*inn*	les insectes	*insects*
l'auberge de jeunesse *f.*	*youth hostel*	le lac	*lake*
la chambre d'hôte	*bed and breakfast*	la nuit	*night*
l'étoile	*star*	décider	*to decide*
la ferme	*farm*	louer	*to rent*
le gîte	*full-service rental cottage*	passer	*to spend (time)*

RECORDING

1.   *Listen to these two couples deciding where they are going to spend the night.*

un hôtel quatre étoiles	*a four-star hotel*
Ça te convient?	*Does that suit you?*
donnant sur (la mer/la rue)	*overlooking (the sea/the street)*
Que tu es exigeant(e)!	*How demanding you are!*
On pourrait louer …	*We could rent …*
Moi non plus.	*Me neither.*

2.

Listen to the details of these hotels and check their facilities.

	Hôtel de la Poste	Hôtel Superbe	Hôtel Bellevue	Grand Hôtel	Hôtel des Pêcheurs
Family suites					
Twin beds					
Single bed					
Bath					
Shower					
TV					
Phone					
Pool					
Fitness/ Gym					
Garage/ Parking					

Quel hôtel préférez-vous?
Which hotel do you prefer?

Lequel préférez-vous?
Which one do you prefer?

le salon
living room

hors de la ville
outside of town

Did You Know?

Most French hotels are controlled by the **Office du Tourisme** and are awarded stars according to their standards; the more stars, the better (and the more expensive) the hotel. There are many hotel chains, e.g., **Formule I**, **Campanile**, **Ibis**, **Mercure**.

Logis de France are family-owned hotels known for their more personal and regional flavor.

Les gîtes ruraux are full-service country cottages or apartments for rent.

Chambres d'hôte are rooms in private homes offering breakfast. Most towns have an official campsite, as well as many private campsites, which will be well equipped and managed. In the peak season, especially in August, it's essential to make reservations early, as many places are booked from year to year.

3. **A vous!** *Find two things to say about each hotel.*

L'hôtel de la Poste   est/n'est pas _____.

a/n'a pas de _____.

L'hôtel Superbe   est/n'est pas _____.

a/n'a pas de _____.

L'hôtel Bellevue   est/n'est pas _____.

a/n'a pas de _____.

Le Grand Hôtel   est/n'est pas _____.

a/n'a pas de _____.

L'hôtel des Pêcheurs   est/n'est pas _____.

a/n'a pas de _____.

RECORDING

4. *Listen to find out which hotel this couple prefers. What reason do they give? Match each hotel with the phrase used to describe it.*

a.	trop petit	Hôtel de la Poste
b.	idéal	Hôtel Superbe
c.	trop bruyant	Hôtel Bellevue
d.	trop cher	Grand Hôtel
e.	trop grand	Hôtel des Pêcheurs

Il n'y a qu'une étoile.   *There's only one star.*

RECORDING

5. **A vous!** *Now you practice saying which hotel you prefer and why. Listen and repeat each phrase.*

Quel hôtel préférez-vous? Pourquoi?

Je préfère l'hôtel _____ parce qu'il est/a _____.

RECORDING 6.

Listen to these people at the hotel reception asking if there are any rooms available. What are they asking for?

Avez-vous une chambre libre?   *Do you have a vacancy?*

une chambre pour deux personnes   *a double room*

RECORDING 7.

A vous! *The clerk is asking you some questions. How would you answer them? Listen and complete the dialog.*

Receptionist: Bonsoir monsieur, madame.

You: (Ask if they have a room free tonight.)

Receptionist: Oui. Pour deux personnes?

You: _____.

Receptionist: Vous restez combien de jours?

You: _____.

Receptionist: Votre nom, s'il vous plaît?

You: _____.

Receptionist: Pouvez vous épeler?

You: _____.

Receptionist: Signez ici. Vous avez une voiture?

You: _____.

Receptionist: Le garage est au sous-sol. Le code du parking est 34 77. Votre numéro d'immatriculation, s'il vous plaît?

You: _____.

Receptionist: Chambre numéro 243, au deuxième étage, l'ascenseur est là-bas. Voilà la clé.

Pronunciation

RECORDING

Listen and repeat the names of these hotels after Jacques:

l'hôtel de la Poste

l'hôtel Superbe

l'hôtel Bellevue

le Grand Hôtel

l'hôtel des Pêcheurs

Now ask where they are:

Pour aller à l'hôtel de la Poste, s'il vous plaît?

Où se trouve l'hôtel Superbe?

L'hôtel Bellevue est au bord du lac?

Le Grand Hôtel est loin d'ici?

Il faut combien de temps pour aller à l'hôtel des Pêcheurs?

Close-up

Rappel! *To make a negative in French you add* **ne** *(or* **n'** *before a vowel) in front of the verb and* **pas** *after the verb:*

Vous êtes suisse?

Non, je ne suis pas suisse.

Il est japonais?

Non, il n'est pas japonais.

When you say there isn't something in French you add **de** *(of/any) after the negative and leave out the word for "the" or "a":*

Il n'y a pas de piscine.

There isn't (a) swimming pool.

Je n'ai pas de femme.

I don't have (a) wife.

Yes and no

Avez-vous une voiture?

Do you have a car?

Oui, j'en ai une.

Yes, I have one (of them).

Non, je n'en ai pas.

No, I don't have one (of them).

Vous n'avez pas de voiture?

You don't have a car?

Oui, c'est vrai. Je n'ai pas de voiture.

Yes, that's right. I don't have a car.

Si, j'en ai une!

Yes (indeed), I do have one!

Vous voulez un hôtel de luxe?

Do you want a luxury hotel?

Pas du tout!

Not at all!

Checkpoints

*Use the check list to test what you've learned in this unit
and review anything you're not sure of.*

Can you ... ?

	Yes	No
• *say where you like to go*	☐	☐

J'aime aller au bord de la mer.
J'aime aller à la campagne.

• *say where you are going on vacation this year* — Yes ☐ No ☐

Cette année je vais à/en ...

• *say who you are going with* — Yes ☐ No ☐

J'y vais avec mon mari/ma femme.
J'y vais avec mon copain/ma copine.
J'y vais avec mon petit ami/ma petite amie.

• *say where you went last year* — Yes ☐ No ☐

Je suis allé(e) à/en ...
On est allé ...

• *say you stayed at home* — Yes ☐ No ☐

Je suis resté(e) à la maison.
On est resté à la maison.

• *say what you like doing* — Yes ☐ No ☐

J'aime faire de la planche à voile.
J'aime jouer au tennis.

• *say you don't like sunbathing* — Yes ☐ No ☐

Je n'aime pas me faire bronzer.

• *say you would like to go rafting* — Yes ☐ No ☐

J'aimerais faire du rafting.

• *say you have never been paragliding* — Yes ☐ No ☐

Je n'ai jamais fait de parapente.

• *say you have tried once/twice* — Yes ☐ No ☐

J'ai essayé une fois/deux fois.

• *say you prefer the hotel with a pool* — Yes ☐ No ☐

Je préfère l'hôtel avec piscine.

• *say the hotel is too big/small/expensive* — Yes ☐ No ☐

L'hôtel est trop grand/petit/cher.

Can you ... ?	Yes	No
• *say what kind of room you want*	☐	☐

une chambre pour une personne
une chambre pour deux personnes avec douche
avec un grand lit
à deux lits
pour deux nuits

	Yes	No
• *reserve a room*	☐	☐

Je voudrais une chambre pour ...

Learning tips

Remember, always try to read aloud. Put your hands over your ears so that you can hear yourself even if you speak very quietly. Try it!

Do you want to learn more?

If you have access to the Internet, you should be able to find tourist information in French as well as in English. Otherwise, French or Canadian tourist offices may be able to give you some brochures in French. See how much you can understand and how many of your favorite vacation pursuits you can name in French.

For more practice, see Extra! on page A4.

U nit 4 is about where you work. You are going to learn some formal language in order to:

- arrange a meeting and use the phone
- recognize and describe people
- talk about the weather
- talk about money

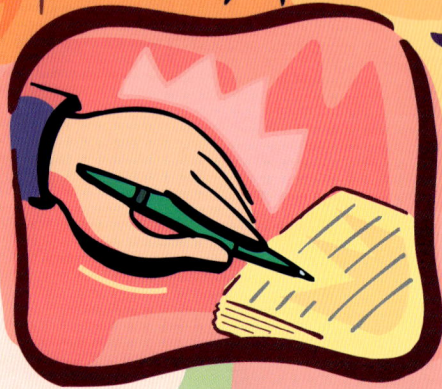

Au travail

4

Word Bank

l'adjoint(e)	*assistant*	la présentation	*presentation*
l'agenda *m.*	*diary*	le rendez-vous	*appointment*
le chef	*head (of department)*	la réunion	*meeting*
le client	*customer*	le service	*department*
la comptabilité	*accounts (department)*	la société anonyme (SA)	*incorporated company*
la conférence	*conference*	la standardiste	*switchboard operator*
les coordonnées	*telephone number*	l'usine *f.*	*(big) factory*
le dîner	*dinner*	la visite	*visit*
le discours	*talk*	le vol	*flight*
l'entreprise *f.*	*firm/company*	le voyage d'affaires	*business trip*
l'usine	*(small) factory*	assister à	*to attend*
le PDG (le président directeur général)	*the CEO*	proposer	*to suggest*
le personnel	*staff*	rentrer	*to return*
le poste (de téléphone)	*(telephone) extension*		

Le personnel

Staff

 é è ê

accent aigu **accent grave** **accent circonflexe**

ç -

cédille **trait d'union**

RECORDING

1. *Who's who at the Société Bonchoix? Listen and fill in the names of some of the members of the staff.*

Le chef du service technique

_____

Le chef comptable

_____

Le PDG

L'adjointe du PDG

_____

Le chef du service marketing

_____

2.

Listen to these telephone conversations. Some of the people to whom the caller wants to speak can't come to the phone. What reasons are given, and when can the caller telephone again? Listen again and check your answers.

Pourrais-je parler à … ?	*Could I speak to … ?*
n'est-ce pas?	*isn't it?*
Ne quittez pas.	*Hold on.*
C'est de la part de qui?	*Who is speaking?*
Je regrette.	*I'm sorry.*
Il/elle n'est pas là.	*He/she isn't there.*
Il/elle est en réunion.	*He/she's in a meeting.*
avec un client	*with a client*
en communication	*on the other line*
en voyage d'affaires	*on a business trip*
parti(e) déjeuner	*at lunch*
pris(e), occupé(e)	*busy (lit: taken)*
Voulez-vous patienter?	*Would you like to hold?*
Je vous le/la passe.	*I'm putting you through to him/her.*

3.

*Tell Sylvie the names of the people at **Imprimat**, and choose five to practice spelling. (Tip: Replace the names with names of people you know and practice spelling them.)*

le PDG	*M. Vincent*
l'adjointe du PDG	*Mme Daniaud*
le chef du service marketing	*M. Thibault*
le chef du service technique	*M. Chaudron*
le chef du personnel	*Mlle Martineau*
la standardise	*Mlle Carriou*

Who has a meeting with whom and when? Listen and draw a line to join the right people and times.

Mr. Haydn-Jones	Mr. Weston	Mr. Bradshaw	Ms. Walker
M. Leclerc	Mme Sibbille	M. Varin	Mme Yon
mardi	mercredi	jeudi	vendredi
10h30	11h20	14h30	15h

Complete the text and then read it back aloud.

a. _____ a rendez-vous avec _____ à
_____ heures.

b. _____ a rendez-vous avec _____ à
_____ heures.

c. _____ a rendez-vous avec _____ à
_____ heures.

d. _____ a rendez-vous avec _____ à
_____ heures.

You're trying to make an appointment to meet M. Dubarry. His secretary reads you what is in his diary for this week. Listen and fill it in.

Lundi
MATIN
APRÈS-MIDI

Mardi
MATIN
APRÈS-MIDI

Mercredi
MATIN
APRÈS-MIDI

Jeudi
MATIN
APRÈS-MIDI

Vendredi
MATIN
APRÈS-MIDI

6.

A vous! *This is your diary. Tell M. Dubarry's secretary what is on your schedule and when you are free to meet him.*

Mon.	
	arrive at Ch. de Gaulle 14:55.
	Transfer to Hotel Bellevue
Tues.	
A.M.	*free*
P.M.	*visit to Electofans, factory tour*
Wed.	
A.M.	*meeting with technical services of Electofans*
P.M.	*free*
Thurs.	
A.M.	*presentation at Pub SA*
P.M.	*free*
Fri.	
A.M.	*appointment with MD Electofans*
P.M.	*depart Ch. de Gaulle 15:45*

Pronunciation

Now practice saying names, job titles, and some other useful telephone phrases after Sylvie and Jacques.

Pourrais-je parler au PDG, M. Gaston?

Pourrais-je parler à l'adjoint du PDG, Mme Hivet?

Vous pouvez me passer le chef du service marketing, M. Guinard?

Vous pouvez me passer le chef du service technique, M. Pinchon?

Je voudrais parler avec M. Lecuyer, le chef de la publicité.

Je voudrais parler avec le chef comptable, Mme Catillon.

Ne quittez pas.

Voulez-vous patienter?

Ma femme? Je vous la passe.

Mon mari? Je vous le passe.

Close-up

Direct object pronouns

<u>me</u>—*me*	<u>nous</u>—*us*
<u>te</u>—*you*	<u>vous</u>—*you*
<u>le/la</u>—*him/her*	<u>les</u>—*them*

Je vous <u>le</u> passe.   *I am putting him through.*

Word order

You already know that reflexive pronouns come <u>in front of</u> the verb:

Je <u>me</u> lave.   *I wash myself.*

Vous <u>vous</u> levez.   *You get (yourself) up.*

Direct object pronouns also come <u>in front of</u> the verb:

me	Il <u>m'</u>entend.	*He can hear me.*
te	Je <u>te</u> comprends.	*I understand you.*
le/l'	Jean? Je <u>le</u> vois.	*Jean? I (can) see him.*
la/l'	La pomme? Tu <u>l'</u>as mangée?	*The apple? Did you eat it?*
nous	Il <u>nous</u> a invités.	*He invited us.*
vous	Il ne <u>vous</u> a pas invités.	*He didn't invite you.*
les	Les enfants? Ils <u>les</u> ont laissés à la maison.	*The kids? They left them at home.*

Notice that in the perfect tense, with <u>avoir</u>, the past participle agrees with the object pronoun. So you add **e** if the pronoun is feminine, **s** if it is masculine plural, and **es** for the feminine plural. As the ending is not normally sounded in conversation you do not need to worry about it.

M. Dubarry arrive

Mr. Dubarry is coming

Word Bank

les affaires	*belongings, "things"*	le parapluie	*umbrella*
l'anorak *m.*	*anorak*	le téléphone portable	*cell/mobile phone*
les baskets	*sneakers*	le porte-documents	*briefcase*
le chemisier	*blouse*	le sac	*bag*
la casquette de base-ball	*baseball cap*	le grand sac de sport	*carryall*
la chemise	*shirt*	le tailleur	*suit (for women)*
le costume	*suit (for men)*	environ	*about*
en costume cravate	*in a shirt and tie*	toujours	*always*
les gants	*gloves*	frisé(e)	*curly*
l'imperméable *m.*	*raincoat*	mince	*thin*
le manteau	*coat*	ondulé(e)	*wavy*
le motif	*pattern*	permanenté(e)	*permed*
l'ordinateur portatif *m.*	*laptop*	raide	*straight*
le pantalon	*pants*	organiser	*to organize*

Listen to these descriptions and decide who you are meeting.

a.   b.   c.   d.

Que puis-je dire?	*What can (should) I say?*
les couleurs vives	*bright colors*
sûr de soi	*sure of himself/self-confident*
à peu près	*about*
Il/elle sourit beaucoup.	*He/she smiles a lot.*
C'est facile de le/la reconnaître.	*It is easy to recognize him/her.*
parce que	*because*
si grand(e)	*so tall*

A vous! *Sylvie is meeting these people. Describe them to her so that she can recognize them.*

Gordon Brown

Lucy Stockwell

M. Dubarry has lost his things. Which are his? Listen and find out.

lequel/laquelle/lesquels/lesquelles?
which one(s)?

celui-ci/celle-ci/ceux-ci/celles-ci
this one here/these ones here

celui-là/celle-là/ceux-là/celles-là
that one there/those ones there

Vous avez vraiment eu de la chance, monsieur!
You're in luck, sir! (lit: you have really had luck)

RECORDING
4.

Jacques is reading out the weather forecast for the day.
*Listen and draw a line to join each region to its
appropriate weather conditions.*

Dans...		
le nord	il pleut et il y a du vent	*it's raining and windy*
le sud	il fait beau	*it's nice*
l'ouest	il y a du soleil/il fait chaud	*it's sunny/it's hot*
l'est	il fait froid	*it's cold*
les Alpes	il y a du brouillard	*it's foggy*
les Pyrénées	il neige	*it's snowing*
le Pas-de-Calais	il y a des orages	*there are storms*

Quel temps fait-il?

What's the weather like?

5.

A vous! *Now you say what the weather is like in the States.*

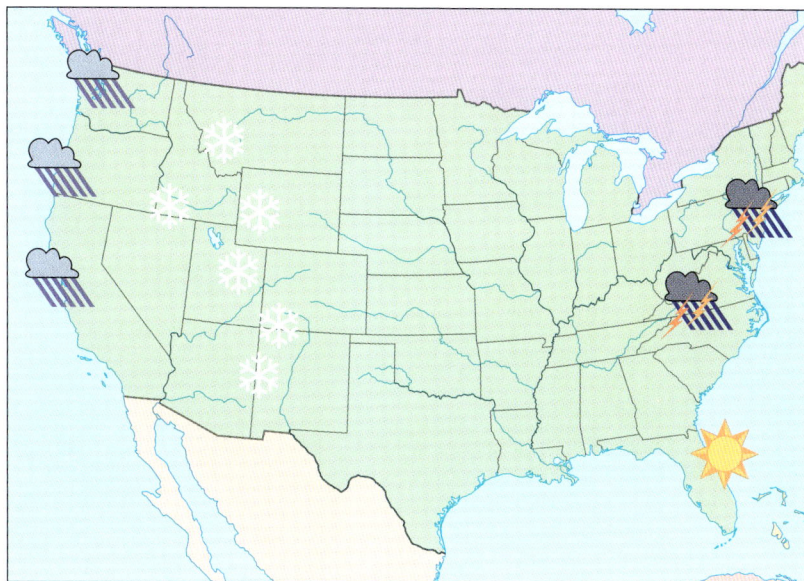

a. Dans le sud _____.

b. Dans l'ouest _____.

c. Dans l'est _____.

d. Dans les Rocheuses _____.

6.

Look at these pictures and decide what the weather is going to be like.

a.   b.   c.   d.

Quel temps fera-t-il?	*What is the weather going to be like?*
Il va faire …	*It is going to be …*
Il va pleuvoir/neiger.	*It is going to rain/snow.*
Il y aura …	*There will be …*

Pronunciation

*Listen to Sylvie and Jacques talking about the weather and really try to copy their accents and intonation. Remember that **t** and **d** at the end of the word are not pronounced.*

Quel temps fait-il?

il pleut

il y a du vent

il fait beau

il y a du soleil

il fait chaud

il fait froid

il y a du brouillard

il neige

il y a des orages

Quel temps fera-t-il?

il va pleuvoir

il y aura du vent

il va faire beau

il y aura du soleil

il va faire chaud

il va faire froid

il y aura du brouillard

il va neiger

il y aura des orages

Close-up

Describing people

Il est grand/petit/de taille moyenne.
He is tall/small/average.

Elle est grande/petite/de taille moyenne.
She is tall/short/average.

Il/elle a les cheveux longs/courts/mi-longs.
He/she has long/short/shoulder-length hair.

Il/elle a les cheveux raides/frisés/ondulés/permanentés/teints.
He/she has straight/curly/wavy/permed/colored hair.

Il/elle a les cheveux blonds/châtain/roux/bruns.
He/she has blonde/chestnut/red/dark brown hair.

Il/elle a les yeux bleus/marron/gris/bleu-gris.
He/she has blue/brown/grey/blue-grey eyes.

Il/elle porte ...
He/she is wearing/wears ...

Which one? This one/that one

These pronouns change to agree in number and gender with the nouns they replace.

	singular		plural	
	m.	f.	m.	f.
Which one?	Lequel?	Laquelle?	Lesquels?	Lesquelles?
This one/these	Celui-ci	Celle-ci	Ceux-ci	Celles-ci
That one/those	Celui-là	Celle-là	Ceux-là	Celles-là

L'argent

Money

W o r d   B a n k

la banque	bank	la pièce (d'un euro)	(€1) coin
le billet (de cinq euros)	(€5) bill	la pièce d'identité	identity card
le Chronopost	express mail	la carte bancaire	banker's card
la commission	commission, charge	la note	hotel bill
la devise	currency	le taux de change	exchange rate
le distributeur automatique	ATM	le traveller/le chèque de voyage	traveler's check
l'horodateur m.	parking meter	régler	to settle (a bill)
la monnaie	change		

RECORDING

1. *Listen to this conversation at the bank and number these sentences in the order in which you hear them.*

Deux cents dollars.

Bonjour madame. Je voudrais changer des chèques de voyage.

Dollars.

Il y a une commission à payer?

Pas pour les chèques de voyage.

A vous! *Now you try exchanging 500 dollars into euros. Complete the dialog and practice reading it aloud, then listen and answer the bank clerk's questions.*

Bank clerk: Bonjour monsieur/madame. Vous désirez?

You: *(Say good morning, I'd like to change some traveler's checks.)*

Bank clerk: Quelle devise?

You: *(Dollars.)*

Bank clerk: Combien?

You: *(500.)*

Bank clerk: Vous avez une pièce d'identité?

You: *(Say yes, here it is.)*

Bank clerk: Un instant. Bon, signez ici.

You: *(Ask if there is a fee to pay.)*

Bank clerk: Pas pour les chèques de voyage.
Au revoir monsieur/madame.

Listen to these exchanges. Then, after each letter, tell how much money is needed.

a. *Pour une chambre?*

b. *Pour l'horodateur?*

c. *Pour une télécarte?*

d. *Pour acheter des timbres?*

4. Listen to these customers at the post office. What do they want? Put the number of the speaker beside each item.

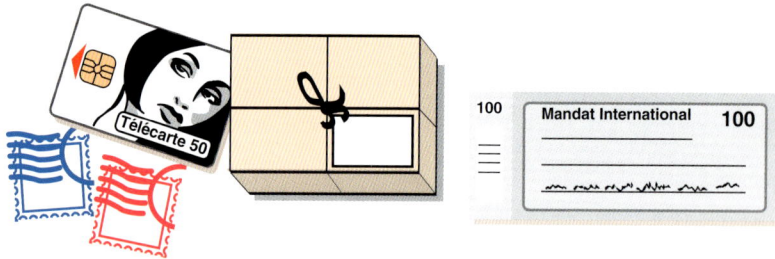

5. For most French public telephones you need to have a **Télécarte**, which you can buy at a post office or newsstand. These are some of the instructions you may see. Match the phrases.

a. Décrochez.

b. Introduisez la carte.

c. Fermez le volet.

d. Patientez SVP.

e. Numérotez.

f. Numéro appelé.

1. *Insert the card.*

2. *Lift receiver.*

3. *Dial the number.*

4. *Number dialed.*

5. *Close the shutter.*

6. *Wait, please.*

Pronunciation

Let's have more practice at pronouncing some useful words and phrases. Listen and repeat after Jacques and Sylvie.

une carte bancaire

un chèque de voyage

un chèque bancaire

J'ai perdu ma carte bancaire.

Je veux changer un chèque de voyage.

Vous prenez les chèques bancaires?

Here's a useful phrase:

Où est-ceque je peux changer de l'argent?   *Where can I change some money?*

Now you are all set for your visit to France.   **Au revoir et bon voyage!**

Close-up

Here are some more useful words and phrases you might see on machines.

Distributeur de billets
ATM

Faites l'appoint.
Put in the exact change.

L'appareil ne rend pas la monnaie.
No change given.

Appuyez sur le bouton.
Press the button.

Attendez.
Wait.

Tapez le code (du parking).
Key in the code (for the car park).

Poussez.
Push.

Tirez.
Pull.

Checkpoints

Use the check list to test what you've learned in this unit
and review anything you're not sure of.

Can you ... ?

Yes   No

- *ask to speak to the CEO M. Dumas* .... ☐ ...... ☐
  Pourrais-je parler au PDG, M. Dumas?

- *ask to speak to his assistant* .... ☐ ...... ☐
  ou à son adjoint(e)

- *ask for extension number 27* .... ☐ ...... ☐
  poste 27

- *say who you are and spell your name* .... ☐ ...... ☐
  C'est de la part de ...

- *ask if you can leave a message* .... ☐ ...... ☐
  Je peux laisser un message?

- *suggest a meeting for Tuesday at 11:00* .... ☐ ...... ☐
  Je vous propose un rendez-vous mardi à onze heures.

- *say you are busy/free* .... ☐ ...... ☐
  Je suis pris(e)/libre.

- *say you will be in a meeting Tuesday morning* .... ☐ ...... ☐
  Mardi matin, je suis en réunion.

- *describe someone so they can be recognized* .... ☐ ...... ☐
  Il est grand/elle est petite.
  Il a les cheveux longs et blonds et porte un jean et des baskets.
  Elle a les cheveux marron courts et porte un tailleur rouge.

- *say you have lost your umbrella* .... ☐ ...... ☐
  J'ai perdu mon parapluie.

- *ask what the weather is like* .... ☐ ...... ☐
  Quel temps fait-il?

- *describe the weather* .... ☐ ...... ☐
  Il fait beau mais il va pleuvoir et il y aura des orages.

- *talk about money* .... ☐ ..... ☐

  Je voudrais changer un traveller.

  Je voudrais changer des dollars.

  Je voudrais régler ma note.

  Excusez-moi. Avez-vous de la monnaie?

  une pièce de deux euros

  un billet de dix euros

Learning tips

Think of all the things you have said in your own language in the last few hours. How many of them were questions? Probably most of them! Now think of yourself arriving in France or another French-speaking country. What are you going to want to say? Where is the ...? Do you have a ...? How do I get to ...? How do you do? Have you been waiting long? Would you like a drink? What time is it? When ...? Imagine that you have just arrived and decide whether you are there as a tourist, on business, or to visit a friend or colleague. Make a list of ten questions you are going to need and practice them until you are really fluent.

Do you want to learn more?

Look up the French names of the items around your home or office in a dictionary. Then write out name tags in French and attach them to the items. Self-adhesive notes are ideal for this, as they are easy to peel off.

For more practice, see Extra! on page A5.

U nit 5 is about your home. You will become familiar with the language you need to know in order to:

- say where it is
- say what it is like and how long you have lived there
- and what rooms there are

Chez moi

5

Word Bank

la banlieue	*suburbs*	beau/belle	*nice, beautiful*
le centre	*center*	près de	*near (to)*
la grande surface	*large store*	loin de	*far (from)*
l'hypermarché *m.*	*large supermarket*	à côté de	*beside*
le marché	*market*	en face de	*opposite*
le quartier	*neighborhood*	entre	*between*
la ville	*town*	à deux minutes de	*two minutes from*
le supermarché	*supermarket*		
ancien/ne	*very old*	écouter	*to listen*

Chez moi

My home

RECORDING

1. *Listen to these people talking about where they live.*

Où habitez-vous?	*Where do you live?*
chez moi	*at my house*
au centre-ville	*in town*
en banlieue	*in the suburbs*
près du centre-ville	*near the center of town*
à la campagne	*in the country*
dans un village	*in a village*

RECORDING

2. *Listen to these young men saying where their houses are and choose the phrase that is most appropriate for each.*

C'est en face de l'église.	*It's opposite the church.*
C'est près de la poste.	*It's near the post office.*
C'est à côté de la pharmacie.	*It's next to the drugstore.*
C'est à deux minutes du supermarché.	*It's two minutes from the supermarket.*
C'est entre la banque et la boulangerie.	*It's between the bank and the bakery.*
C'est où exactement?	*Where exactly is it?*

3. **A vous!** *Now can you say where these houses are?*

a.

b.

c.

4.

Now listen to find out whether these men like living where they do and what reasons they give. Match the speaker with the appropriate phrase.

C'est comment?
What is it like?

a. **C'est un quartier très calme.**   *It's a very quiet neighborhood.*

b. **Il y a du monde.**   *There are a lot of people.*

c. **C'est bruyant. Il y a beaucoup de circulation.**   *It's noisy. There's a lot of traffic.*

d. **C'est un petit hameau ancien.**   *It's a little old hamlet.*

e. **Il y a de belles propriétés.**   *There are some beautiful houses.*

5.

Listen to find out how they get to the shops. Match the speaker with the appropriate method of transportation.

a. **On prend le bus.**

b. **On y va à pied.**

c. **J'y vais en voiture.**

d. **J'y vais à bicyclette.**

Pronunciation

RECORDING

Listen and repeat the phrases after Jacques. Would you recognize the places or neighborhoods if someone said them to you in those phrases? Listen again and check.

Now repeat these questions.

Où habitez-vous?

C'est où exactement?

C'est comment?

Pour aller en ville?

Close-up

Notice how these words and expressions are followed by **de** *(of):*

près <u>de</u>	*near to*
loin <u>de</u>	*far from*
à côté <u>de</u>	*beside*
en face <u>de</u>	*opposite*
à deux minutes <u>de</u>	*two minutes from*

Rappel!

	m.	f.	pl.
(de + le) =	<u>du</u>	<u>de la</u>	(de + les) = <u>des</u>
	<u>de l'</u>	<u>de l'</u>	

Some place names which include **le**, **la**, *or* **les** *also follow this rule:*

J'habite près <u>du</u> Havre.	*I live near Le Havre.*
C'est loin <u>du</u> Mans.	*It's far from Le Mans.*

Val-Thorens est à côté <u>des</u> Menuires.
Val-Thorens is next to Les Menuires.

C'est près <u>de La</u> Haye.	*It's near the Hague.*

C'est à deux minutes <u>des</u> Halles.
It's two minutes from Les Halles.

C'est en face <u>du</u> Mont-Blanc.	*It's opposite Mont Blanc.*

Ma maison

My house

Word Bank

l'appartement *m.*	*apartment*	le jour	*day*
l'immeuble *m.*	*apartment building*	le mois	*month*
le jardin	*garden/yard*	la semaine	*week*
le lotissement	*housing development*	joli/e	*pretty*
la maison	*house*	moderne	*modern*
le pavillon	*detached house*	vieux/vieille	*old*
l'an *m.*	*year*		

RECORDING

1. *Listen and find out who lives in which house. Match the picture with the number of the speaker.*

a.

b.

c.

d.

e.

What are the houses like? Listen to find out.

Rappel!

assez   *quite*   très   *very*

Listen to find out which floor these people live on.
Draw a line from each person to the appropriate floor.

M. and Mme Dubois

Mlle Fourrier

M. Simon

La famille Bourjeout

Jacqueline

La famille Bertrand

Nicolas

le lapin de Nicolas

au rez-de-chaussée	*on the ground floor*
au premier étage*	*on the 1st floor*
au deuxième étage	*on the 2nd floor*
au troisième	*on the 3rd*
au quatrième	*on the 4th*
au cinquième	*on the 5th*
au sixième	*on the 6th*
au septième	*on the 7th*
au huitième	*on the 8th*
dernier/dernière	*last*
dans le grenier	*in the attic*
au sous-sol	*in the basement (lit: below ground)*

*Unlike the United States, in France, the first floor is the level above the ground floor.

4.

How long have they been living there? Listen and find out.

Vous habitez ici depuis combien de temps?
How long have you lived here?

Vous y habitez depuis combien de temps?
How long have you lived there?

depuis	*since/for*
depuis un mois	*for a month*
depuis deux ans	*for two years*

5.

A vous! *Now it's your turn to say where you live. First answer Sylvie's questions, then practice asking them yourself.*

Où habitez-vous?   **J'habite …**

C'est quelle sorte de maison?   **C'est …**

Vous y habitez depuis combien de temps?
J'y habite depuis …

Pronunciation

The letter "h" at the beginning of a word is not pronounced. Listen and repeat these words and phrases after Sylvie.

l'hôtel

Pour aller à l'hôtel, s'il vous plaît?

l'hôpital

L'hôpital est tout près.

J'habite à Tokyo et j'y habite depuis deux ans.

Mon frère habite à La Haye, en Hollande.

Ma sœur habite au Havre, en France.

Close-up

Rappel! *All nouns are masculine or feminine. Adjectives used with feminine nouns mostly add **e**:*

m.	f.
grand	grand<u>e</u>
joli	joli<u>e</u>
petit	petit<u>e</u>

Irregular adjectives

Some adjectives have different endings for the feminine:

m.	f.
ancien	ancien<u>ne</u>
beau	be<u>lle</u>
blanc	blan<u>che</u>
vieux	vie<u>ille</u>

L'appartement est grand/petit/vieux/ancien/beau/joli
La maison est grande/petite/vieille/ancienne/belle/jolie

Depuis

*In French when you are talking about how long you have been doing something you use **depuis** (since/for) and the PRESENT tense:*

J'<u>habite</u> ici <u>depuis</u> cinq ans
I have been living here for five years.

J'<u>apprends</u> le français <u>depuis</u> deux mois.
I have been learning French for two months.

Je <u>sors</u> avec lui <u>depuis</u> l'année dernière.
I have been going out with him since last year.

A la maison

At home

Word Bank

l'armoire *f.*	*wardrobe*	la machine à laver	*washing machine*
l'ascenseur *m.*	*elevator*	les meubles	*furniture*
la baignoire	*bathtub*	le miroir	*mirror*
le balcon	*balcony*	les petites annonces	*classifieds*
le canapé	*sofa*	la pièce	*room*
la chambre	*bedroom*	la porte	*door*
la commode	*chest of drawers*	la rivière	*stream*
la cuisine	*kitchen*	la salle	*room*
la cuisinière	*stove*	la salle de bains	*bathroom*
la douche	*shower*	le salon	*sitting room*
l'emplacement *m.*	*space, spot*	la salle de séjour	*living room*
l'entrée *f.*	*entrance*	la salle à manger	*dining room*
l'escalier *m.*	*stairs*	les toilettes	*toilet/bathroom*
le fauteuil	*armchair*	la vue	*view*
la fenêtre	*window*	chaque	*each*
le frigidaire/frigo	*fridge*	acheter	*to buy*
le garage	*garage*	donner	*to give*
le lave-vaisselle	*dishwasher*	donner sur	*to look on to*
le lit	*bed*	faire une liste	*to make a list*

Listen to find out who lives where. Put the right number by each floorplan.

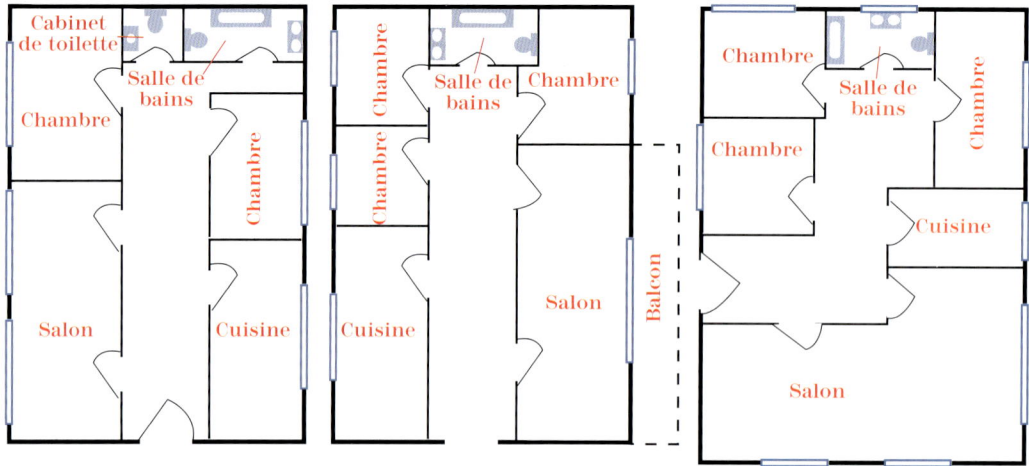

Cabinet de toilette	Salle de bains	Chambre
Chambre		Chambre
Salon	Cuisine	

a.

Chambre	Chambre	Salle de bains	Chambre
Chambre			
Cuisine		Salon	Balcon

b.

Chambre	Salle de bains	Chambre
Chambre		Cuisine
Salon		

c.

Jacques and Sylvie are apartment-hunting together. Listen and check the things they say they need, then write in the number of bedrooms they want.

à louer	*for rent*
Qu'est-ce qu'il leur faut?	*What do they need?*
Ça suffit.	*That's enough.*
C'est trop cher.	*It's too expensive.*
Moi aussi.	*Me too.*
Ah non, ça alors!	*Certainly not!*

DidYouKnow?

When talking about their houses the French often say how many rooms they have (excluding the bathroom and kitchen), so **un trois pièces** would have two bedrooms and a living room, **un quatre pièces** would have three bedrooms and a sitting room, and so on.

3. *Read these ads and see how many words you know.*

L'ISLE ADAM	33 Bord estuaire Gironde	2PIÈCES 45 M²
Maison 4 chbres, s. à manger, salon avec cheminée, cuis. et salle de bains équipées, gar., 1.700m2 clos, €380.000 Part. tél	Girondine restaurée 150m2, jard., gar., ponton 16/57.46.16.00	PROX M° BALARD 44.19.62.62

Offres vides 3ᵉ

2PIÈCES 45 M²
PROX M° BALARD
44.19.62.62

-METRO CRIMEE-
4P. 74 M2 - €212.000

Appartements
Maisons
ventes, province

St MARTIN
PRES BEAUBOURG
A LOUER
4P. s/cour, 90m2, refait
neuf, 2e ét. asc., cave.
€1650 + €40 ch part.
(1)45.27.50.34 répondeur

TOULON
Quartier résidentiel, bord
de mer. Part. vend
magnifique F4, gd séjour/s.
à manger, 2 chbres, co-ppté
gd stand. avec parc
arboré et piscine,
€280.000

VILLA A HYERES

RECORDING

4. *Now you are being shown around the apartment. Listen and write down which room you are being shown by the real estate agent.*

Il y a de la place pour …
There is room for …

RECORDING

5. *Listen and check the items of furniture that Jacques and Sylvie still need to buy.*

Il y avait …	There was …
Il n'y avait pas de …	There wasn't a …
Tu es sûr(e)?	Are you sure?
J'en suis sûr(e).	I am sure (of it).
Il y en avait un(e).	There was one (of them).
Ça suffit pour le moment.	That's enough for the moment.

Pronunciation

The accent circonflexe is often used over a vowel which would be followed by an "s" in related words in English. Listen and repeat these phrases.

août *(August)*

Les vacances sont au mois d'août.

arrêt *(stop)*

Où est l'arrêt d'autobus?

château *(castle)*

Le château de Versailles est très beau.

fête *(feast/festival)*

Bonne fête!

île *(isle)*

On fait une excursion aux îles d'Hyères.

Close-up

Il faut

We have already come across the expression **il faut**, *meaning it is necessary:*

<u>Il faut</u> aller en ville pour trouver un hôtel.

Il faut *can also be used to say you need something:*

Il <u>me</u> faut un stylo à bille.	*I need a ballpoint pen. (lit: it is necessary to me)*
Il <u>te</u> faut un fauteuil.	*You need an armchair. (lit: to you)*
Il <u>lui</u> faut un plan de la ville.	*He/she needs a town map. (lit: to him/her)*
Il <u>nous</u> faut un frigidaire.	*We need a fridge. (lit: to us)*
Il <u>vous</u> faut un billet.	*You need a ticket. (lit: to you)*
Il <u>leur</u> faut un horaire des trains.	*They need a train schedule. (lit: to them)*

En

When you say "I have one" in French you must add **en** *(of it, of them) in front of the verb:*

Avez-vous des crayons?	Oui, j'<u>en</u> ai un.
Do you have any pencils?	*Yes, I have one (of them).*
Est-ce qu'il y a une table?	Oui, il y <u>en</u> a une.
Is there a table?	*Yes, there is one (of them).*

Different ways of saying "yes"

oui	*yes*
oui, d'accord	*yes, I agree (lit: agreed)*
si*	*yes, I do*

*** Si** *is used after negative questions:*

Vous ne voulez pas le frigo?	<u>Si.</u>
You don't want the fridge?	*Yes, I do.*

Rappel! <u>De</u> *after the negative:*

Il y a ...	*There is/are ...*
Il n'y a pas <u>de</u> ...	*There isn't/aren't (a/any) ...*

Checkpoints

Use the check list to test what you've learned in this unit
and review anything you're not sure of.

Can you ... ?
        Yes   **No**

- **say where you live** .... ❑ ...... ❑

  J'habite en ville.

  J'habite à la campagne.

- **say where something is** .... ❑ ...... ❑

  C'est en face de l'église.

  C'est près de la poste.

  C'est à côté de la pharmacie.

  C'est à deux minutes du supermarché.

  C'est entre la banque et la boulangerie.

- **say you live in a house/apartment** .... ❑ ...... ❑

  J'habite dans une maison/un appartement.

- **say on which floor someone lives** .... ❑ ...... ❑

  Il/elle habite au rez-de-chaussée.

  Il/elle habite au premier étage.

- **say you have lived there (two) years** .... ❑ ...... ❑

  J'y habite depuis (deux) ans.

- **say the house is nice** .... ❑ ...... ❑

  La maison est belle.

- **say there is** .... ❑ ...... ❑

  Il y a une cuisine et une salle de bains.

  Il y a un salon/une salle de séjour.

  Il y a trois chambres.

  Mais il n'y a pas de salle à manger.

  Il y a un frigo.

  Mais il n'y a pas de lit.

Learning tips

Creating "associations" often helps you to remember new words:

chambre	*chamber*
jour	*journal (daily paper)*
an/année	*annual*
lit	*litter (a "carrying bed" or a lot of puppies asleep!)*
maison	*mansion*

Can you think of some more to help with these words?

dormir	*to sleep*
premier	*first*
ville	*town*
fille	*girl*

Do you want to learn more?

When you look up a word in a French-English dictionary, make sure to read all the meanings. A single word, depending on its context, will have several different meanings. So when you want to say something in French, think of how you're going to use the word you need to look up, then check the various usages listed.

For more practice, see Extra! on page A8.

LA GARE

Unit **6** is about long-distance travel using public and private transportation. After completing this unit you will be able to:

- talk about a trip you have taken and arrange to rent a car
- make arrangements to travel by train
- get around with your own or a rental car

En voyage

6

W o r d   B a n k

l'arrivée *f.*	*arrival*	le réseau	*network*
l'assurance *f.*	*insurance*	la route	*the road*
l'avion *m.*	*plane*	le supplément	*supplement*
le billet	*ticket*	le train	*train*
le car	*long-distance bus*	compris(e)	*included*
le départ	*departure*	de bonne heure	*early*
la durée	*length of time*	en retard	*late*
le guichet	*ticket office*	avec une demi-heure de retard	*half an hour late*
les heures de pointe	*peak times (rush hour)*	souvent	*often*
le permis de conduire	*driver's license*	conduire	*to drive*
la pièce d'identité	*identity card*	*venir	*to come*

Arrivée en France

Arriving in France

RECORDING 1.

Some people you met on vacation in Cannes are telling you how they got there. Listen to find out what method of transport they used, then write down the time taken for each trip. Notice the use of the perfect tense to say when they arrived.

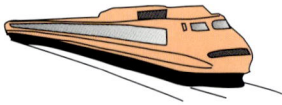      

| en train | en car | en moto | en voiture | en avion |

Durée   _____ heures   _____ heures   _____ heures   _____ jours   _____ jours

Il y a (une heure/deux jours).
(An hour/two days) ago.

RECORDING 2.

Listen to find out when they left and when they arrived in Cannes.

	Départ	Arrivée
mercredi	_____ heures	_____ heures
jeudi	_____ heures	_____ heures
vendredi	_____ heures	_____ heures
samedi	_____ heures	_____ heures
aujourd'hui	_____ heures	_____ heures

DidYouKnow?

Beaune *is a historic town in the Bourgogne region famous for its red wine.* **Avignon** *is a medieval town in Provence which was once the seat of the Pope.* **Grenoble** *is a historic town centrally situated in the Alps.* **La route Napoléon** *is the route across the southern Alps used by Napoleon on his return from exile. The* **TGV (train à grande vitesse)** *is a very fast express train, for which seats have to be reserved in advance.*

RECORDING 3.

A vous! *Now it's your turn to tell your French friends about your trip. Prepare what you would say using the perfect tense, then practice saying it aloud. Listen to check your answers.*

a. Je suis venu(e) …

b. Je suis parti(e) …

c. Je suis arrivé(e) …

New York	dép.	mardi 18.00
Paris Roissy	arr.	mercredi 7.00
Paris Gare de Lyon	dép.	vendredi 14.45
Lyon Perrache	arr.	vendredi 17.15
Lyon Perrache	dép.	dimanche 11.15
Cannes	arr.	dimanche 14.15

RECORDING 4.

Simon has just flown in from New York to Paris Charles-de-Gaulle. At the information desk, what methods of transport is he advised to take to get to downtown Paris? What are the advantages and disadvantages of each? Listen to find out.

| Métro | RER | Roissy bus | Taxi |

RECORDING 5.

This person wants to rent a car. Listen and answer the questions.

a. *What sort of car does she want?*

b. *For how many people?*

c. *For how long?*

d. *What does the agent ask for?*

e. *What does she have to pay extra for?*

f. *How does she pay?*

g. *Where is the car?*

A vous! *Now you practice renting a car. Listen and be prepared to answer the questions!*

You: (Say you want to rent a car.)

Clerk: Quelle sorte de voiture?

You: (You want a big one for four people.)

Clerk: Pour combien de jours?

You: (A week.)

Clerk: Vous avez votre pièce d'identité et votre permis de conduire?

You: (Say yes, here they are.)

Clerk: Vous payez comment?

You: (Ask if he takes Master Card.)

Clerk: Oui, bien sûr.

You: (Ask him if he has a map of the town.)

Clerk: Oui, les voilà.

You: (He's forgotten to tell you where the car is. Better ask.)

Clerk: Oh, excusez-moi, c'est dans le parking là-bas, emplacement A5.

Pronunciation

Repeat the parts of the verb **venir** *in the present tense.*

Now practice the perfect tense.

Je suis venu(e) en train.　　　　　**Nous sommes venu(e)s à deux.**

Tu es venu(e) en avion.　　　　　**Vous êtes venu(e)(s) mercredi?**

Il est venu en moto.　　　　　　　**Ils sont venus en voiture.**

Elle est venue à pied.　　　　　　**Elles sont venues en car.**

Close-up

Venir

Present tense

*venir—to come

je viens	nous venons
tu viens	vous venez
il vient	ils viennent
elle vient	elles viennent

Perfect tense

je suis venu(e)	nous sommes venu(e)s
tu es venu(e)	vous êtes venu(e)(s)
il est venu	ils sont venus
elle est venue	elles sont venues

on est venu(e)　　　*we came*

On prend le train

We're taking the train

Word Bank

la gare	*station*	après-demain	*the day after tomorrow*
le quai	*platform*	prochain(e)	*next*
un aller-retour	*a round-trip ticket*	composter	*to validate a ticket*
un aller simple	*a one-way ticket*	rater	*to miss*

RECORDING

1. **Listen to this woman giving information about train times and write them in.**

	train 1	train 2	train 3
a. Lyon			
b. Caen			
c. Nice			
d. Lille			
e. Nantes			

Le train part à quelle heure?	*What time does the train leave?*
Il faut changer.	*You have to change.*
Il y en a un autre.	*There is another (train).*
trop tôt	*too early*
attendez	*just a moment (lit: wait)*

Listen to these conversations to find out: a. which train
these people choose; b. which platform it leaves from;
c. when it gets in; and d. whether they have to change.
Fill in the table.

Destination	départ	quai	changement à	arrivée
Lyon				
Caen				
Nice				
Lille				
Nantes				

Le train pour Caen part de quel quai?	Which platform does the Caen train leave from?
Vous savez?	Do you know?
Je regrette.	I'm sorry.
Vous l'avez raté.	You've missed it.
Vous pouvez …	You can …

A vous! *How much does each passenger pay
and where are they going?*

Ticket Price	Destination
1. €_____	_____
2. €_____	_____
3. €_____	_____

DidYouKnow?

To book a ticket in France you
can use **Minitel**, a public
service database that is
accessed through the home
telephone. Alternatively you can
use **Socrate**, a program
available on automatic
ticket machines at most
mainline stations.

Which tickets are these people buying? Listen and put the right number by each ticket.

| SNCF | Pour être valable, ce titre doit être composté lors de l'accès au train | ALLER-RETOUR | Résa | Classe 2 |

Départ 18.58 PARIS — Départ 07.32 LONDRES — Train 4060 — Voiture 03
01 Places 25 — Références
Arrivée 21.24 LONDRES — Arrivée 10.45 PARIS
Date LE 16.06.03 — Date LE 20.06.03
Valid du **DEPART TRAIN EN PERIODE BLEUE** — Prestations — Réduct. — Nombre — Prix
Particularités
1 HAUT
€53,00

a.

| SNCF | Pour être valable, ce titre doit être composté lors de l'accès au train | ALLER SIMPLE | Résa | Classe 2 |

Départ 13.12 PARIS — Train 2070 — Voiture 09
01 Places — Références
Arrivée 16.24 BRUXELLES
Date LE 14.04.03
Valid du **DEPART TRAIN EN PERIODE ROUGE** — Prestations — Réduct. — Nombre — Prix
Particularités
€19,50

b.

| SNCF | Pour être valable, ce titre doit être composté lors de l'accès au train | ALLER-RETOUR | Résa | Classe 1 |

Départ 20.30 PARIS — Départ 10.23 CANNES — Train 5061 — Voiture 07
01 Places 65 — Références
Arrivée 07.41 CANNES — Arrivée 23.39 PARIS
Date LE 10.04.03 — Date LE 24.04.03
Valid du **DEPART TRAIN EN PERIODE BLANCHE** — Prestations — Réduct. — Nombre — Prix
Particularités
1 HAUT
COUCHETTE 00 01
ENFANT 02 01
€89,60

c.

| SNCF | Pour être valable, ce titre doit être composté lors de l'accès au train | ALLER-RETOUR | Résa | Classe 1 |

Départ 20.30 PARIS — Départ 10.23 CANNES — Train 5061 — Voiture 07
01 Places 65 — Références
Arrivée 07.41 CANNES — Arrivée 23.39 PARIS
Date LE 10.04.03 — Date LE 24.04.03
Valid du **DEPART TRAIN EN PERIODE BLANCHE** — Prestations — Réduct. — Nombre — Prix
Particularités
1 HAUT
COUCHETTE 00 01
ADULTE 00 01
€179,00

d.

A vous! *Practice what you would say to buy a round-trip ticket to London. Listen and answer the ticket officer's questions.*

Ticket officer: Bonjour monsieur/madame.

You: (Say good morning.)

Ticket officer: Vous désirez?

You: (Say you want to go to London, a round-trip ticket.)

Ticket officer: Vous devez réserver. Vous voulez en première ou deuxième classe?

You: (First class.)

Ticket officer: Fumeur ou non fumeur?

You: (Non-smoking.)

Ticket officer: Vous voulez partir quand?

You: (Tomorrow evening.)

Ticket officer: Demain soir.

RECORDING

6. *There's been a delay. Listen and check how late the trains are.*

ARRIVEE   Paris–Gare de Lyon

En provenance de

Lyon ___19.45___ _____

Marseille ___20.32___ _____

Dijon ___20.56___ _____

Le train a du retard.	*The train is late.*
en provenance de	*from*
être retardé	*to be delayed*

RECORDING

7. *You're going to be late arriving from Dijon. You'd better phone the hotel to let them know when you are due to get in—fortunately there is a phone on the train. Make sure you have your* **carte de téléphone***!*

Mme Ribault à l'appareil.	*Mme Ribault speaking.*
de	*from*
A ce soir!	*See you this evening.*

Pronunciation

First practice repeating the future tense of **arriver** *and* **aller** *after Sylvie, then repeat these phrases after Jacques.*

J'arriverai lundi.
Tu arriveras à quelle heure?

Il arrivera après moi.
Elle arrivera en retard.

Nous arriverons à la gare du Nord.
Vous arriverez à la place de la République.

Ils arriveront après-demain.
Elles arriveront de bonne heure.

Now make up your own phrases to use with the future tense of **aller** *and practice saying them aloud.*

J'irai	**Nous irons**
Tu iras	**Vous irez**
Il ira	**Ils iront**
Elle ira	**Elles iront**

Close-up

To say at what time you use **à**:

Le train part à onze heures dix et arrive à quatorze heures vingt.
The train leaves at 11:10 and arrives at 14:20.

À quelle heure?   *At what time?*

The future tense

Sylvie uses the future tense to say when she will arrive:

J'ai du retard. J'arriverai à midi.   *I am late. I will arrive at noon.*

Sylvie a du retard. Elle arrivera vers huit heures.
Sylvie is late. She will arrive about eight.

Le train a du retard. Il arrivera avec une demi-heure de retard.
The train is late. It will arrive about half an hour late.

In the future tense the endings are regular for all verbs. To form the future you add the endings to the infinitive of the verb.

arriver—*to arrive*

j'arriverai	nous arriverons
tu arriveras	vous arriverez
il arrivera	ils arriveront
elle arrivera	elles arriveront

Some irregular verbs have a stem change.

aller—*to go (stem changes to ir)*

j'irai	nous irons
tu iras	vous irez
il ira	ils iront
elle ira	elles iront

You are unlikely to need to use the future tense as much as the near future. The near future (futur proche) is used more in conversation to talk about future events. However, you should be able to recognize it.

The other most common irregular verbs are:

avoir—*to have*	j'aurai
faire—*to do/make*	je ferai
venir—*to come*	je viendrai
être—*to be*	je serai
pouvoir—*to be able*	je pourrai
voir—*to see*	je verrai

En voiture

Traveling by car

Word Bank

l'agglomération *f.*	built-up area		le rond-point	rotary, traffic circle
l'aire de repos *f.*	unsupervised rest area (usually with toilets and picnic tables)		la route nationale	main road
			la route départementale	minor road
l'autoroute *f.*	highway		la station-service	gas station (with shop and refreshments or restaurant)
le bouchon	traffic jam (lit: cork)			
le carrefour	intersection		la voie	(traffic) lane
les clignotants	blinkers (turn signals)		arrêter	to stop
			céder (le passage)	to yield
les embouteillages	traffic jam (lit: bottlenecks)		doubler	to pass
les feux	traffic lights		mettre (les clignotants)	to switch on (the turn signals)
la limite de vitesse	speed limit		payer	to pay
le panneau	road sign		ralentir	to slow down
le péage	toll		rouler	to drive (lit: to roll)
la place	square		suivre	to follow
le pont	bridge			

RECORDING 1.

Listen to the advice these people are being given and trace their routes on the highways.

RECORDING 2.

These visitors want to know the way to the local supermarket. Listen and choose the right sketch.

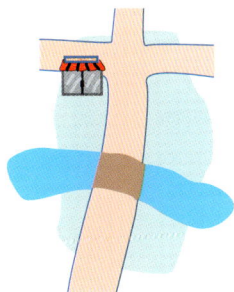
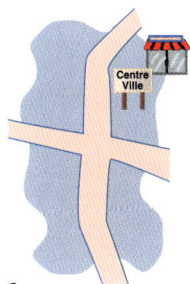
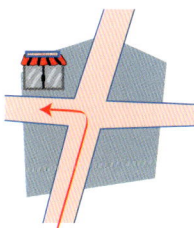
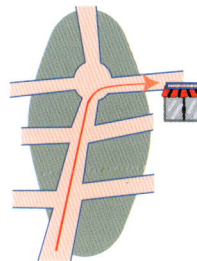

a.   *b.*   *c.*   *d.*   *e.*

A vous! *Now it's your turn to give Sylvie the same directions.*

Allez …	*Go …*
Continuez …	*Continue …*
Prenez …	*Take …*
Suivez …	*Follow …*
Tournez …	*Turn …*

Listen and write down what the speed limits are.

a. Sur les autoroutes, c'est _____ kilomètres à l'heure.

b. Sur les routes à 4 voies, c'est _____ kilomètres à l'heure.

c. Sur les autres routes, les routes nationales et les départementales, c'est _____ kilomètres à l'heure.

d. En ville et en agglomération, c'est _____ kilomètres à l'heure.

Anne-Laure is learning to drive. What is her instructor telling her to do?

Mais non!	*No!*
Dis donc!	*Look (here)! Hey!*
Ah, voilà!	*Ah, there you are/that's it.*
Zut alors!	*Damn!*
Allez-y.	*Go on.*
Ça va déjà mieux.	*That's (already) better.*

Did You Know?

Highways in France are called **autoroutes** and drivers have to pay to use most of them. A warning sign, **Péage,** indicates when you are entering the paying part of the system. You are normally instructed to take a ticket (**prenez un billet**) on entering and to pay at the **Péage** on leaving the highway.

Highway numbers are preceded by A (**Autoroute**) and highway signs are blue. The numbers of main roads are preceded by N (**Nationale**) and minor road numbers by D (**Départementale**). You may see a route marked by a green **Itinéraire: Bis** or **Itinéraire du Bison Futé** sign. This indicates an alternative route avoiding highways and built-up areas. The signs are often accompanied by a picture of a bison (**bison futé** means the cunning bison).

6. RECORDING

A vous! *Now you tell Sylvie to do the same things, without the expletives!*

7. *What do you think these signs mean? Pair up the words with the appropriate sign.*

a.

b.

c.

d.

Cédez le passage *(Yield)*

Virages dangereux *(Dangerous curves)*

Passage piétons *(Pedestrian crossing)*

Passage à niveau *(Railroad crossing)*

Chanssée glissante *(Slippery)*

Rétrécissement *(Road narrows)*

Travaux *(Work zone)*

e.

f.

g.

Pronunciation

RECORDING

Listen and practice giving the commands in the Close-up.

Close-up

Giving orders

Infinitive	**Vouvoyer** *(using the **vous** form)*
arrêter	Arrêtez au feu rouge.
céder	Cédez le passage.
continuer	Continuez tout droit.
doubler	Doublez.
prendre	Prenez la deuxième rue à gauche.
ralentir	Ralentissez.
rouler	Roulez moins vite.
tourner	Tournez à droite.

Checkpoints

Use the check list to test what you've learned in this unit
and review anything you're not sure of.

Can you ... ?

	Yes	No
• *say how you traveled*	❑	❑
Je suis venu(e) en avion.		
Je suis venu(e) en train.		
Je suis venu(e) en voiture.		
• *say you left (15:00 Tuesday)*	❑	❑
Je suis parti(e) (mardi à 15 heures)		
• *say you arrived (19:00 Wednesday)*	❑	❑
Je suis arrivé(e) (mercredi à 19 heures)		
• *say you want to rent a car*	❑	❑
Je veux louer une voiture.		
• *say for two people*	❑	❑
Pour deux personnes.		
• *ask if you can pay by credit card*	❑	❑
Je peux payer avec une carte de crédit?		
• *ask when the train to Paris leaves*	❑	❑
Le train pour Paris part à quelle heure?		
• *say the train arrives at 12:00*	❑	❑
Le train arrive à Boston à midi.		
• *tell someone they have to transfer*	❑	❑
Il faut changer.		
• *ask for a round-trip ticket to Lyon*	❑	❑
Un aller-retour pour Lyon.		
• *say smoking/non-smoking*	❑	❑
Fumeur/non fumeur.		
• *tell the hotel you have a room reserved*	❑	❑
J'ai réservé une chambre.		
• *say that your train is late*	❑	❑
Le train a du retard.		
• *say that you will arrive at 11 P.M.*	❑	❑
J'arriverai à vingt-trois heures.		

Can you ... ?

Yes   No

- *give directions* . . . . ❑ . . . . . . ❑
  Allez tout droit.
  Tournez à gauche au carrefour.
  Tournez à droite aux feux.
  Suivez les panneaux.

- *give instructions* . . . . ❑ . . . . . ❑
  Arrêtez.
  Ralentissez.
  Doublez.
  Cédez le passage.

Learning tips

Build up your own list of useful phrases to help you out of any difficulties and spend some time practicing them. Here is a starter kit:

Comment?	*Pardon?*
Encore!	*More!*
Pouvez-vous répéter cela?	*Could you repeat that?*
Parlez plus lentement, s'il vous plaît.	*Please speak more slowly.*
Je ne comprends pas.	*I don't understand.*
Je n'ai pas compris.	*I didn't understand.*
Je n'ai rien compris.	*I didn't understand a thing.*
Parlez-vous anglais?	*Do you speak English?*
Excusez-moi.	*Excuse me.*

Do you want to learn more?

Read as much French as you can find—newspapers, advertising brochures, whatever. Read a little at a time, and don't worry about bits you don't understand. Concentrate on getting the gist. Once you know what the subject is, you'll be able to guess the meanings of many new words from their context. Keep a note of words that are the same or similar in French and English, but look in your dictionary to check that the meaning is the same.

For more practice, see Extra! on page A8.

le chat	*cat*
la chevelure	*head of hair*
le choix	*choice*
l'essence *f.*	*gas*
le goût	*taste*
la soie	*silk*
le savon	*soap*
sans	*without*
tant (de)	*so many*
chauve	*bald*
doux/douce	*soft*
impeccable	*perfect*
meilleur(e)	*best*
brûler	*to burn*
choisir	*to choose*
faire pénétrer	*to rub in*
grossir	*to get fat*
laisser	*to leave*
rouler	*to go (by vehicle)*

RECORDING

1. *Listen to the recording and identify what products are being sold in the television advertisements.*

RECORDING

2. *Listen to the recording and determine how long each of these promotions will last.*

Vous aurez une belle chevelure.	*You'll have a fine head of hair.*
Votre choix sera impeccable.	*Your choice will be perfect.*

2 Extra!

le contenu	*contents*
la moutarde	*mustard*
le persil	*parsley*
le plat à four	*baking dish*
le poivre	*pepper*
le sachet de levure	*packet of baking powder*
le saladier	*mixing bowl*
le sel	*salt*
à four chaud	*in a hot oven*
dedans	*inside*
haché	*chopped*
ramolli	*softened*
râpé	*grated*
ajouter	*to add*
beurrer	*to butter/grease*
cuire	*to cook*
mélanger	*to mix*
verser	*to pour*

RECORDING

1. *Listen to the recording and fill in the missing quantities on the list of ingredients.*

Un gâteau au jambon

Il faut:

_____ oeufs

_____ cuillerées à soupe bien pleines de farine

_____ de jambon

_____ de beurre ramolli

_____ de gruyère râpé

_____ cuillerées à soupe de moutarde

_____ persil haché

_____ sachet de levure

_____ sel et du poivre

2.

Listen to the recording for activity 1 again and put the instructions listed below in the correct order.

a. Cuire à four chaud pendant environ trois quarts d'heure (thermostat 6–7).

b. Beurrer un plat à four et verser le tout dedans.

c. Verser le contenu du petit saladier dans le grand. Ajouter le jambon et mélanger le tout.

d. Dans un grand saladier, mélanger la farine, la levure et le gruyère.

e. Dans un petit saladier, mélanger les œufs, le persil, la moutarde, le beurre, le sel et le poivre.

3 Extra!

Listen to find out what these people are packing.
Where do you think they're going on vacation?

Where do these people want to go on vacation?

4 Extra!

Une lettre ou télécopie pour réserver une chambre.
A letter or fax to reserve a room.

> L'Hôtel Les Deux Sapins
> Bois Vert
>
> Monsieur,
>
> Je voudrais réserver une chambre pour deux personnes avec salle de bains et donnant sur le lac, du 14 au 21 juin.
>
> Je vous serais reconnaissant(e) de bien vouloir m'indiquer vos prix.
>
> En vous remerciant d'avance, je vous prie de croire, Monsieur, à l'expression de mes sentiments distingués.
>
> J. Clouseau

1. *Write a letter of your own; reserve two rooms with twin beds, bath, and television for four people from July 16 to 25.*

donnant sur …	*overlooking (lit: giving on to)*
Je vous serais reconnaissant(e) de bien vouloir m'indiquer vos prix.	*I would be most grateful if you could let me know what your prices are.*
En vous remerciant d'avance …	*Thanking you in advance …*
Je vous prie de croire, Monsieur, à l'assurance de mes sentiments distingués./Veuillez agréer, Monsieur/Madame, l'assurance de mes sentiments distingués.	*Yours faithfully*

A shorter form often used when sending a fax is:

Meilleures salutations	*Best wishes*

2. *Read the reply from the hotel.*

> Cher M. Dixon,
>
> Suite à votre lettre du 12 avril, le peux vous offrir une chambre pour deux personnes avec salle de bains et balcon donnant sur le lac au premier étage, et une chambre avec douche et WC donnant sur le lac mais sans balcon, au troisième étage. Toutes nos chambres sont équipées d'une télévision et du téléphone. J'attends votre confirmation avant de faire vos réservations.
>
> Ci-joint des brochures avec nos prix et des informations sur la région.
>
> En attendant votre réponse, je vous prie d'agréer, monsieur, mes salutations distinguées.

suite à	*following*
Toutes nos chambres sont équipées de …	*All our rooms are equipped with*
ci-joint	*enclosed*

3. *Send a fax or letter confirming the reservation.*

Je voudrais confirmer la réservation …

4. *Monique has been staying with you. Read and translate the letter she has written.*

Cher Jon, chère Amanda,

Je vous remercie de nouveau de votre gentille hospitalité. Les vacances aux Etats-Unis étaient vraiment magnifiques. En vous quittant, on a passé encore une semaine à New York pour voir les gratte-ciel, les musées, les théâtres et bien sûr les magasins. C'était vraiment impressionnant. Nous voulons revenir dans deux ans pour faire un tour des parcs nationaux. Vous voulez faire un tour avec nous?

Quand on est arrivé chez nous, il pleuvait et il faisait un froid terrible. J'étais très fatiguée, avec le long voyage et le décalage horaire, et j'ai dormi pendant 18 heures. La prochaine fois que vous venez en France, il faut absolument nous rendre visite.

Je vous envoie des photos que j'ai prises pendant le séjour chez vous.

Amicalement

Monique

cher/chère	dear
de nouveau	again
gentil(le)	kind
l'hospitalité	hospitality
magnifique	magnificent
En vous quittant …	When we left you … (lit: on leaving you)
encore un(e) …	another
la semaine	week
le gratte-ciel	skyscraper
vraiment	really
impressionnant	impressive
le parc national	national park

fatigué(e)	tired
le décalage horaire	time change
pendant	for, during
La prochaine fois que vous venez …	Next time you come …
le séjour	stay
Amicalement	With friendly greetings
envoyer	to send
passer	to spend
remercier	to thank
rendre visite	to visit
revenir	to return
voir	to see
J'étais	I was
il faisait froid	it was cold
il pleuvait	it was raining

5 Extra !

RECORDING

1. *Listen to find out which chest of drawers is bought.*

    a.   *b.*   *c.*

RECORDING

2. *Make a list of the furniture the couple decides to buy for a new apartment.*

6 Extra !

RECORDING

1. *Listen to the recording and choose the appropriate highway sign for each situation.*

    a.   *b.*   *c.*

Test 1

Review of Units 1-2

1. *Reflexive verbs. Put in the correct form of the reflexive pronoun.*

1. Je _____ lève

2. Ils _____ lavent

3. Elle _____ réveille

4. Nous _____ habillons

5. Comment tu _____ appelles?

6. Vous _____ levez à quelle heure?

2. *Fill in the missing verb.*

1. Je me _____ à six heures et demie.

2. Je me _____ à sept heures.

3. Je _____ une douche.

4. Je me _____ les cheveux.

5. Je m' _____ .

6. Je _____ mon petit déjeuner.

7. Je _____ du thé au citron.

8. Je _____ de l'exercice.

9. Je _____ de la maison à sept heures et demie.

10. J'_____ au travail à huit heures.

arriver

boire

faire

habiller

se lever

manger

prendre

se réveiller

sècher

partir

3. *Complete the verbs.*

avoir

J'ai		nous _____	
tu _____		vous _____	
il _____		ils _____	

être

Je suis		nous _____	
tu _____		vous _____	
il _____		ils _____	

4. *Make the past participle.*

Regular verbs:

1. aller
2. manger
3. répondre
4. rendre
5. finir
6. sortir

Irregular verbs:

7. boire
8. prendre
9. faire
10. ouvrir

5. *Find these people a suitable snack.*

1. J'ai faim.
2. J'ai soif.
3. J'ai chaud.
4. J'ai froid.
5. Je fais un régime.
6. Je suis diabétique.

a. Voilà du chocolat bien chaud!
b. Voulez-vous une glace?
c. Voici une pression.
d. Nos glaces sont faites avec de l'édulcorant.
e. Voici un steak frites.
f. Je vous propose une salade niçoise.

6. **Du, de la, de l'**, *or* **des?** *Fill in the correct form.*

1. La poste est près _____ banque.

2. Le château est loin _____ centre.

3. L'hôtel est à côté _____ magasins.

4. Le restaurant est en face _____ hôtel.

5. La station de métro est à deux minutes _____ supermarché.

7. *What does the pharmacist suggest?*

1. J'ai une grippe.

2. J'ai mal à la tête.

3. Je suis enrhumé(e).

4. J'ai mal à la gorge.

5. Je me suis coupé un doigt.

a. de la crème antiseptique et un pansement

b. des pastilles et des mouchoirs en papier

c. des suppositoires

d. un sirop et des comprimés

e. des analgésiques

8. **Cherchez l'intrus.** *Find the odd one out.*

1. l'armoire; la commode; le frigidaire

2. le jardin; la cuisine; le salon

3. le canapé; le lit; le fauteuil

4. le pavillon; la fenêtre; la porte

5. la douche; la salle de bains; l'entrée

6. l'immeuble; la salle; la maison

9. *Describing people. Choose the right endings for talking about a woman.*

1. a. grand, b. grande

2. a. petite, b. petit

3. a. paresseux, b. paresseuse

4. a. active, b. actif

5. a. beau, b. belle

6. a. vieux, b. vieille

10. *Complete the dialog.*

1. Bonsoir monsieur/madame.

2. Oui. Pour combien de personnes?

3. A deux lits ou un grand lit?

4. Vous restez combien de temps?

5. Oui, bien sûr.

6. Le garage est au sous-sol. Vous avez la chambre numéro 56.

a. Avez-vous un parking?

b. Deux personnes

c. Bonsoir. Avez-vous une chambre de libre?

d. Un grand lit

e. Trois nuits

f. Avez-vous une chambre avec salle de bains?

Test 2

Review of Units 3–6

1. *More verbs ... Regular verbs, present tense. Put the right endings on the verbs:*

-er

J'arriv___   nous arriv___

tu arriv___   vous arriv___

il arriv___   ils arriv___

-re

Je répond___   nous répond___

tu répond___   vous répond___

il répond___   ils répond___

-ir

je fini___   nous fini___

tu fini___   vous fini___

il fini___   ils fini___

2. *Which verb do they go with in the past tense?* **Avoir** *or* **être**?

1. aller
2. avoir
3. faire
4. jouer
5. manger
6. partir
7. répondre
8. venir

3. *Complete the dialog.*

1. Bonjour monsieur/madame.
2. Vous désirez?
3. En première ou seconde?
4. Fumeur ou non fumeur?
5. Vous voulez partir quand?

a. Demain soir.
b. Bonjour madame.
c. Non fumeur.
d. Première.
e. Un aller-retour pour Paris.

4. *Give the imperative form of these verbs.*

1. aller—*to go*

2. continuer—*to continue*

3. prendre—*to take*

4. suivre—*to follow*

5. tournez—*to turn*

5. **Cherchez l'intrus.** *Find the odd one out.*

1. l'ail, le beurre, le fromage

2. le bœuf, l'agneau, les oignons

3. les tomates, la salade, les fraises

4. le lait, les radis, le yaourt,

5. la dinde, le poulet, les œufs

6. le veau, le porc, le jambon

6. *Put in the right form of* **avoir** *or* **être**.

1. Elle _____ allée en ville.

2. Il _____ eu une grande surprise.

3. J'_____ fait de la planche.

4. Nous _____ joué au basket.

5. On _____ mangé des escargots.

6. Elle _____ partie en retard.

7. Il n'_____ pas répondu.

8. Ils _____ venus en voiture.

7. **Grand ou grande?** *Adjective agreement. Choose the correct form.*

1. Mon appartement est grand/grande.

2. Le jardin est très joli/jolie.

3. La maison est dans une ville ancien/ancienne.

4. Les propriétés *(f)* sont beaux/belles.

5. Les rues *(f)* sont petits/petites.

6. Le pont est vieux/vieille.

8. *What is your excuse? You are answering the phone for Mr. Eastwood. How would you say:*

1.	He isn't there.	*a.*	Il est avec un client.
2.	He's in a meeting.	*b.*	Il est occupé.
3.	He's with a client.	*c.*	Il n'est pas là.
4.	He's on the other line.	*d.*	Je vous le passe.
5.	He's on a business trip.	*e.*	Il est parti déjeuner.
6.	Hold on.	*f.*	Il est en voyage d'affaires.
7.	He's at lunch.	*g.*	Il est en réunion.
8.	He's busy.	*h.*	Il est en communication.
9.	I am putting you through.	*i.*	Ne quittez pas.

9. **On va en vacances avec qui?** *Who are you going on vacation with? Fill in the correct form:* **mon, ma,** *or* **mes.**

1. avec _____ famille

2. avec _____ amis

3. avec _____ ami

4. avec _____ amie

5. avec _____ petite amie

6. avec _____ mari

10. *Choose the right question.*

1. Qu'est-ce que vous aimez faire?

2. Qu'est-ce que vous n'aimez pas faire?

3. Qu'est-ce que vous préférez?

4. Avez-vous jamais essayé de faire du parapente?

5. Qu'est-ce que vous aimeriez essayer?

a. Non, jamais.

b. Je voudrais essayer de faire du parapente.

c. J'adore l'équitation.

d. Je déteste le foot.

e. Je préfère les vacances à la montagne.

11. **Quel temps fait-il?** *Choose the right symbol.*

1. il pleut

a.

2. il y a du vent

b.

3. il y a du soleil

c.

4. il fait chaud

d.

5. il fait froid

e.

6. il y a du brouillard

f.

7. il neige

g.

8. il y a des orages

h.

12. *At the bank. Complete the dialog.*

1. Bonjour monsieur/madame. Vous désirez?

2. Quelle devise?

3. Combien?

4. Vous avez une pièce d'identité?

5. Un instant. Oui, signez ici.

Pas pour les chèques de voyage. Voilà vos euros. Au revoir monsieur/madame.

a. Oui, la voilà.

b. Il y a une commission à payer?

c. Dollars.

d. Deux cents dollars.

e. Bonjour madame. Je voudrais changer des chèques de voyage.

A n s w e r   K e y

Unit 1

Pages 1–4

1. 1. 6:45; 2. 9:00; 3. 8:15; 4. 4:00;
5. 10:30

2. shaving—3; getting up—1; eating breakfast
with family—8; getting dressed—4;
shower—2; buying bread—7; drinking orange juice—5; walking the dog—6

3. a. Elle prend une douche; b. Elle prend son
petit déjeuner; c. Elle se lève; d. Elle se
réveille; e. Elle se sèche les cheveux

4. a. <u>Quelquefois</u> je me lève à sept heures mais
<u>normalement</u> je me lève à six heures.;
b. <u>Normalement</u> je prends une douche, mais
<u>quelquefois</u> je fais du jogging.;
c. <u>Normalement</u> je ne prends pas de petit déjeuner, mais <u>quelquefois</u> je mange une tartine.; d. <u>Normalement</u> je sors à huit heures
mais <u>quelquefois</u> je sors à sept heures.

5. a. nothing, coffee with milk—1; b. croissant,
coffee—2; c. bread, butter, honey, or jam,
coffee—3; d. cereal, margarine, and jam
on bread, tea—4; e. egg, bread, yogurt,
milk—5.

6. Answers will vary.

Pages 6–8

1. 1—nurse; 2—baker; 3—businessman;
4—teacher; 5—store assistant; 6—secretary

2. 1. bed until 11 o'clock and then goes to his
mother's for lunch; 2. sport, soccer in winter
and tennis in summer; 3. bike rides;
4. windsurfing/long walks; 5. restaurant

3. 1.b—a picnic; 2.c—château; 3.d—beach;
4.a—tennis; 5.e—windsurfing; 6.h—a bike
ride

4. 1a. g; 2b. e; 3c. f; 4d. d; 5e. a; 6f. c

5. Answers will vary.

6. On pourrait jouer au tennis; aller à la plage;
aller à Disneyland/au parc d'attractions;
aller au jardin public; faire du shopping;
aller à la piscine; aller au cinéma.

Pages 10–12

1. beach—3; theater—5; town—1; restaurant—
4; tennis—2

2. woke up, 6:00; got up at 6:30; drank
orange juice and read paper, 6:00–6:30;
shower, 6:30; leave for work, 7:30; arrive at
office, 7:55

3. A.M.—got up at eight o'clock and went to town;
She did her shopping and met her boyfriend
Jacques; they went shopping together.

P.M.—fast food outlet and the cinema; then
they went back to her house. She made a
chocolate cake and they drank a cup of tea.

evening—meal in a restaurant with friends

4. Answers will vary.

Unit 2

Pages 18–20

1. 1. 250g of garlic 500g of onions, a kilo of
potatoes, and 200 grams of mushrooms;
Soupe aux champignons

2. Lettuce, 500g of tomatoes, celery,
radishes; salade mixte

3. a cabbage, 500g of carrots, and 50g of
onions; choucroute

2. 1. beef, steak, pork—steak frites

2. beef, steak, Burgundian beef, pork
sausages, game meat—blanquette de
veau

3. no meat, vegetarian—salade niçoise

4. steak, poultry, pork, everything—steak
frites, poulet rôti, frites

5. hamburgers, chicken, steak, fast food—
Poulet rôti frites

3. 1. crème brûlée; 2. on a diet; 3. lemon pie,
allergic to peanuts; 4. strawberry ice cream;
5. chocolate cake

4. J'aime la soupe aux champignons; Je n'aime
pas tellement le poisson; Je ne mange pas de
tomates; Je suis très chocolat; Je suis allergique à l'ail.

5. 1—Bof!; 2—délicieux; 3—délicieux; 4—dégoûtant; 5—insipide

6. Answers will vary.

Pages 22–24

1. 1.La brasserie, Salon de Thé, La Créperie

2. 1. soupe du jour
   2. filet de poisson frais du Bistro
   3. pas de dessert pour moi
   4. la salade variée aux pignons de pin
   5. le steak au poivre

3. Answers will vary.

4. 1. knife; 2. salt; 3. more bread; 4. ashtray; 5. spoon and sugar

5. 1—€37,80; 2—€59,20; 3—€48,60; 4—€31,45; 5—€35

Pages 26–28

1. 1. eaten too much, feels sick; 2. bad back; 3. headache; 4. fallen and hurt knee; 5. cough, sore throat and temperature; 6. toothache

2. a. J'ai mal à la main. J'ai une ampoule.; b. J'ai de la fièvre.; c. J'ai mal au pied.; d. J'ai mal à la tête.; e. J'ai mal aux dents.

3. a. today at 16:20; b. tomorrow at 9:35; c. today at 17:10; d. Friday 10:45; e. call the ambulance: dial 15

4. cough and flu; cough and cold; cut finger

6. 1. tablets to take with water, three times a day before meals; 2. syrup—three tablespoons a day after meals; 3. suppositories to insert one in the evening and one in the morning; 4. antiseptic cream and some bandages; 5. pain killers—take two, four times a day.

Unit 3

Pages 34–37

1. 1. d; 2. a; 3. b; 4. a; 5. c

2. 1. g—Les Ardennes; 2. d—La Côte d'Azur; 3. a—Les Alpes; 4. e—La Bretagne

4. 1. mes copains—my buddies; 2. mon mari—my husband; 3. tout seul—alone; 4. Mon petit ami et mes deux enfants—my boyfriend and my two children; 5. un groupe touristique—a group of tourists

6. Answers will vary.

Pages 40–42

1. 1. hiking, cycling; 2. lying on the beach, getting tan, dancing; 3. windsurfing, cycling, mountain biking, tennis, skiing; 4. swimming, sailing; 5. fishing

2. 1. jogging; 2. tennis, volleyball, group sports, and soccer; 3. lying on the beach and sunbathing; 4. hiking

3. 1. never, it's awful; 2. several times, it's super; 3. once, fantastic; 4. twice, it's great; 5. several times, it's super

4. 1. paragliding, but afraid and it's expensive; 2. diving, tried it once and would like to learn; 3. horseback riding; 4. kayaking and rafting; 5. sailing; 6. paragliding

5. 1. skiing, cross-country skiing; 2. skiing, cross-country skiing, and ice skating; 3. snowboarding; 4. ice hockey and sledding; 5. snowboarding, skiing, cross-country skiing, ice skating, sledding, everything

6. Answers will vary.

Pages 44–48

2.

	Hôtel de la Poste	Hôtel Superbe	Hôtel Bellevue	Grand Hôtel	Hôtel des Pêcheurs
Family suites			✔	✔	
Twin beds					
Single bed					
Bath	✔	✔			
Shower	✔		✔	✔	✔
TV		✔		✔	
Phone					
Pool			✔	✔	✔
Fitness/Gym					
Garage/Parking	✔	✔	✔		

3. Answers will vary.

4. a. Hôtel des Pêcheurs; b. Hôtel Bellevue; c. Hôtel de la Poste; d. Hôtel Superbe; e. Grand Hôtel

5. a. Je préfère l'Hôtel des Pêcheurs parce qu'il est petit.; b. Je préfère l'Hôtel Bellevue parce qu'il est en dehors de la ville.; c. Je préfère l'Hôtel de la Poste parce qu'il est au centre-ville.

6. two double rooms for tonight; a room with a double bed for two nights from 9–11 May;

One double room with a double bed and one with two singles from 12–15 May; A single room for tonight; For the week 14–21 August, one double room and a room with 3 beds; And a room with a shower and a bathroom for tonight and with a crib

7. a. Avez-vous une chambre libre pour ce soir?; b. Oui, une chambre à deux lits, avec douche et poste de télévision.; c. Pour deux nuits.; d. Answers will vary.; e. Answers will vary.; f. Oui. Vous avez un parking?; g. Answers will vary.

Unit 4
Pages 54–57

1. Le PDG, M. Gaston; l'adjointe du PDG, Mme Hivet; Le chef du service marketing, M. Guinard; le chef du Service technique, M. Pinchon; le chef comptable, Mme Catillon

2. 1. M. Gaston in a meeting, after 2 P.M.; 2. Mme Hivet, on the phone, ten minutes; 3. M. Guinard, with a client, half an hour; 4. M. Lecuyer, putting you through; 5. Mme Catillon in a meeting, she will call back if you leave your number.

4. Mr. Haydn-Jones—Mme Yon—vendredi 11:20

Mr. Weston—M. Varin—jeudi 15:00

Mr. Bradshaw—M. Leclerc—mardi 14:30

Ms. Walker—Mme Sibbille—mercredi 10:30

5. Lundi—10 A.M. meeting with chef du service marketing, 2:00 conference

Mardi—A.M. factory visit, P.M. free

Mercredi—A.M. with client, P.M. free

Jeudi—A.M. presentation, P.M. dental appointment

Vendredi—A.M. free, P.M. vacation

Next week—on vacation

6. J'arriverai lundi, Paris-Charles-de-Gaulle à 14h55 et je vais rester à l'hôtel Bellevue.

Mardi matin je suis libre et l'après-midi je fais la visite de l'usine Electofans.

Mercredi matin, j'ai une réunion avec le service technique d'Electofans et l'après-midi est libre.

Jeudi matin j'assiste à une présentation chez Pub S.A. et l'après-midi je suis libre.

Vendredi matin j'ai un rendez-vous avec le PDG de Electofans et l'après-midi je prends l'avion à l'aéroport Charles-de-Gaulle à 15h45 pour rentrer.

Alors je vous propose un rendez-vous mercredi après-midi

Pages 60–63

1. a. M. Proudhon; b. Mme Chaumont; c. Mme Hérault; d. M. Dubarry

2. Gordon Brown, le PDG, a soixante-cinq ans, et il est très grand, à peu près un mètre quatre-vingt-dix. Il a les cheveux gris, et quand il voyage il porte toujours un pantalon beige, un chemise à carreaux, un pull bleu foncé et une casquette de baseball.
Lucy Stockwell porte un polo, un jean, des baskets et un pull.

3. the briefcase; navy blue raincoat; large umbrella with bank logo; leather gloves (not wool)

4. le nord—il pleut; le sud—il y a des orages; l'ouest—il fait beau; l'est—il fait froid; les Alpes—il neige; les Pyrénées—il y a du soleil; le Pas-de-Calais—il y a du brouillard

5. a. Dans le sud il fait du soleil et il fait très chaud; b. Dans l'ouest il pleut; c. Dans l'est il y a des orages; d. Dans les Rocheuses il neige et il fait très froid.

6. a. il va faire beau/il y aura du soleil; b. il va faire froid; c. il va pleuvoir; d. il y aura du vent

Pages 66–68

1. Deux cents dollars (3); Bonjour madame. Je voudrais changer des chèques de voyage. (1); Dollars (2); Il y a une commission à payer? (4); Pas pour les chèques de voyage. (5)

2. Bonjour monsieur/madame. Je voudrais changer des chèques de voyage.
Dollars.
Cinq cents dollars.
Oui, la voilà.
Il y a une commission à payer?

3. a. €84; b. €1; c. €7,40; €14,75; d. €2

4. a. phone card—1; b. two stamps—2; c. send money form—3; d. small parcel—4

5. a. 2; b. 1; c. 5; d. 6; e. 3; f. 4

Unit 5

Pages 74–75

2. 1. two minutes from the supermarket; 2. it's opposite the church; 3. between the bank and the bakery; 4. next to the drugstore; 5. near the post office

3. a. C'est entre la banque et la boulangerie; b. C'est à côté de la pharmacie; c. C'est en face de l'église

4. 1. b; 2. a; 3. d; 4. c; 5. e

5. 1. bus—a; 2. car—c; 3. walk—b; 4. bike—d; 5. car—c

Pages 77–79

1. 1. a—large apartment building in town; 2. b—large house in town; 3. c—apartments in suburbs; 4. d—small house in country; 5. e—small development in suburbs

2. 1. large, modern, nice; 2. big, old; 3. small, old; 4. really old, small, pretty; 5. quite small, very new

3. M. Simon, ground floor; Jacqueline, first floor; La famille Bourjeout, second floor; La famille Bertrand, third floor; M. et Mme Dubois, fifth floor; Mlle Fourrier, eighth floor; Nicolas in the attic; his rabbit in the basement

4. a. M. Dubois—5 years; b. Mlle Fourrier—1 month; c. M. Simm—2 years; d. Mme Bourjeout—9 years; e. Jacqueline—10 months; f. M. Bertrand—3 years; g. Nicolas—2 days

5. Answers will vary.

Pages 82–83

1. a. 2; b. 3; c. 1

2. kitchen, shower, living room, garage, and balcony should be checked; 2 bedrooms

3. L'ISLE-ADAM
4 bedroom house, dining room, living room with fireplace, fully-equipped kitchen and bathroom, garage, fenced 1,700 m2 lot, €380,000. Sale by owner. Call.

APARTMENTS, HOUSES, SALES OUTSIDE PARIS

VILLA IN HYERES
33 (an area of France close to Bordeaux) by the estuary of the Gironde River, traditional restored house, 150 m2 lot, garage, dock tel: 16/57 46 16 00

UNFURNISHED 3RD (a borough of Paris)
St Martin close to Beaubourg
4 rooms on courtyard, 90 m2, completely remodeled, 2nd floor, elevator, basement storage, €1650 + €40 utilities, private landlord 01 45 27 50 34 answering machine

2 rooms 45 m2 close Balard Metro
01 44 19 62 62

Crimee Metro 4 rooms 74 m2 €212,000

TOULON
residential area by the shore. Sale by owner, beautiful four-room apartment, large living room/dining room, 2 bedrooms, luxury condo in wooded park, swimming pool, €380,000

4. 1. kitchen; 2. bedroom; 3. bathroom; 4. living room with balcony; 5. bedroom; 6. basement garage

5. a refrigerator; table for the kitchen; a sofa and armchair; a bed, a wardrobe and a mirror; a chest of drawers

Unit 6

Pages 90–92

1. 1. train, 5 hours; 2. coach, 3 days; 3. motorbike, 7 days a week; 4. car, 10 hours; 5. plane, 1 hour

2. 1. Jeudi, dép 15.30 arr 20.18; 2. Mercredi 8.00, Vendredi 17.00; 3. Samedi, 10.00, yesterday, 16.00; 4. Vendredi 22.00, Samedi, 8.00; 5. ce matin, 11.00, 12.05

3. Answers will vary.

4. the metro or the RER, which is quicker, but it is often very crowded; taxi is fastest but at rush hour there is a lot of traffic and it is expensive; Roissy bus to center of town every twenty minutes and takes about forty minutes.

5. a. not too big (Renault Mégane); b. 1 person; c. 3 days; d. identity card and driver's license; e. insurance; f. American Express; g. in the parking lot (space B7)

6. a. Je veux louer une voiture.
b. Une grande voiture pour quatre personnes.
c. Une semaine.
d. Oui, les voilà.
e. Vous prenez la Master Card?
f. Avez-vous un plan de la ville?
g. Où est la voiture?

Pages 94–97

1.

		train 1	train 2	train 3
a.	Lyon	10:35	14:18	18:05
b.	Caen	9:12	10:43	11:27
c.	Nice	8:19	10:56	11:56
d.	Lille	10:39	13:28	17:18
e.	Nantes	7:22	11:09	13:47

2.

	Destination	dép	quai	change à	arr
a.	Lyon	10:35	5	Dijon	13:05
b.	Caen	10:43	11		11:57
c.	Nice	10:56	7		13:26
d.	Lille	13:28	2		12:18
e.	Nantes	11:09	1	Paris	14:26

3. €26.53 Calais; €92.60 Paris-Cannes; €11 Paris

4. a. 2; b. 1; c. 3; d. 4

5. a. Bonjour.; b. Londres, un aller-retour; c. Première.; d. Non fumer.; e. Demain soir.

6.

Lyon	19:45	2 hours late
Marseille	20:32	1 hour late
Dijon	20:56	due to arrive at 22:14

Pages 101–103

1. 1. A13 to Rouen then A15; 2. A6 to Lyon then A7; 3. A6 towards Beaune and A38; 4. A10; 5. A4; 6. A1 then A26, then tunnel

2. a. 2; b. 4; c. 1; d. 5; e. 3

3. 1. Allez tout droit et tournez à gauche au carrefour.; 2. Allez tout droit, traversez le pont et le voilà sur votre gauche.; 3. Continuez jusqu'au feu et puis et oui, tournez à droite.; 4. Suivez les panneaux centre-ville.; 5. Allez tout droit jusqu'au rond-point et prenez le première sortie.

4. a. 130km/h; b. 110km/h; c. 90km/h; d. 50km/h

5. yield; stop; turn right; pass; slow down; put signals on; stop

6. il faut céder le passage, arrêtez, tournez à droite, doublez, ralentissez, mettez les clignotants, arrêtez

7. a. Cédez le passage; b. Virages dangereux; c. Passage piétons; d. Passage à niveau; e. Chaussée glissante; f. Rétrécissement; g. Travaux

Extra 1
Page A1

1. 1. Rosée du matin (soap); 2. FINO (gasoline); 3. Votre Génération (magazine)

2. 1. one day; 2. two weeks; 3. one week

Extra 2
Pages A2–A3

1. <u>cinq</u> oeufs

<u>cinq</u> cuillerées à soupe bien pleines de farine

<u>200g</u> de jambon

<u>125g</u> de beurre ramolli

<u>100g</u> de gruyère râpé

<u>deux</u> cuillerées à soupe de moutarde

<u>du</u> persil haché

<u>un</u> sachet de levure

<u>du</u> sel et du poivre

2. 1. Dans un petit saladier, mélanger les œufs, le persil, la moutarde, le beurre, le sel, et le poivre.; 2. Dans un grand saladier, mélanger la farine, la levure, et le gruyère.; 3. Verser le contenu du petit saladier dans le grand. Ajouter le jambon et mélanger le tout.; 4. Beurrer un plat à four et verser le tout dedans.; 5. Cuire à four chaud pendant environ trois quarts d'heure (thermostat 6–7).

Extra 3
Page A4

1. Spain

2. 1. United States; 2. Northern Spain; 3. Mexico; 4. Italy

Extra 4
Pages A5–A7

1. Sample answer:

Monsieur,
Je voudrais réserver deux chambres donnant sur le lac avec deux lits chacune, salle de bain et télévision pour quatre personnes du 16 au 25 juillet.

Je vous serais reconnaissant de bien vouloir m'indiquer vos prix.

En vous remerciant d'avance, je vous prie de croire, Monsieur, à l'assurance de mes sentiments distingués.

David Dixon

3. Suite à votre lettre du..., je voudrais confirmer la réservation pour deux chambres du 16 au 25 juillet pour quattre personnes.

Meilleures salutations,

David Dixon

4. Dear John, Dear Amanda,

I want to thank you again for your kind hospitality. Our vacation in the US was really magnificent. When we left you, we spent another week in NYC to see the skyscrapers, museums, the theaters, and, of course, the shops. It was really impressive. We want to return in two years to go for a tour of the national parks. Do you want to go on a tour with us?

When we arrived home, it was raining and terribly cold. I was very tired by the long journey and the time change, and I slept for 18 hours. Next time you come to France, you absolutely have to visit us. I am sending you some pictures I took.

With friendly greetings,

(your name)

Extra 5
Page A8
1. black dresser
2. bedside table; chairs; mirror; lamps; sofa

Extra 6
Page A8
1. 1—a (yield sign); 2—a (historic site sign); 3—b (highway sign)

Test 1
Pages B1–B4
1. 1. me; 2. se; 3. se; 4. nous; 5. t'; 6. vous
2. 1. réveille; 2. lève; 3. prends; 4. sèche; 5. habille; 6. mange; 7. bois; 8. fais; 9. pars; 10. arrive
3. tu as; il a; nous avons; vous avez; ils ont; tu es; il est; nous sommes; vous êtes; ils sont

4. 1. allé; 2. mangé; 3. répondu; 4. rendu; 5. fini; 6. sorti; 7. bu; 8. pris; 9. fait; 10. ouvert
5. 1. e; 2. c; 3. b; 4. a; 5. f; 6. d
6. 1. de la; 2. du; 3. des; 4. de l'; 5. du
7. 1. c; 2. e; 3. b; 4. d; 5. a
8. 1. le frigidaire; 2. le jardin; 3. le lit; 4. le pavillon; 5. l'entrée; 6. la salle
9. 1. b; 2. a; 3. b; 4. a; 5. b; 6. b.
10. 1. c; 2. b; 3. d; 4. e; 5. f; 6. a

Test 2
Pages B5–B10
1. -er

J'arrive	nous arrivons
tu arrives	vous arrivez
il arrive	ils arrivent

-re

Je réponds	nous répondons
tu réponds	vous répondez
il répond	ils répondent

-ir

je finis	nous finissons
tu finis	vous finissez
il finit	ils finissent

2. 1. être; 2. avoir; 3. avoir; 4. avoir; 5. avoir; 6. être; 7. avoir; 8. être
3. 1. b; 2. e; 3. d; 4. c; 5. a
4. 1. Allez!; 2. Continuez; 3. Prenez!; 4. Suivez!; 5. Tournez!
5. 1. l'ail; 2. les oignons; 3. les fraises; 4. les radis; 5. les œufs; 6. le veau
6. 1. est; 2. a; 3. ai; 4. avons; 5. a; 6. est; 7. a; 8. sont
7. 1. grand; 2. joli; 3. ancienne; 4. belles; 5. petites; 6. vieux
8. 1. c; 2. g; 3. a; 4. h; 5. f; 6. i; 7. e; 8. b; 9. d
9. 1. ma; 2. mes; 3. mon; 4. mon; 5. ma; 6. mon
10. 1. c; 2. d; 3. e; 4. a; 5. b
11. 1. c; 2. f; 3. a; 4. e; 5. d; 6. h; 7. b; 8.g
12. 1. e; 2. c; 3. d; 4. a; 5. b